The Prime Ministers from Walpole to Macmillan

Published by
Dod's Parliamentary Companion Limited
PO Box 3700, Westminster, London SW1E 5NP

First published in Great Britain 1994
by Dod's Parliamentary Companion Ltd,
PO Box 3700, Westminster, London SW1E 5NP

ISBN: 0 905702 22 0

Designed and typeset by The Creative Centre Limited, London WC2.
Printed and bound in Great Britain by Redwood Books, Trowbridge, Wiltshire.

Dod's Parliamentary Companion Ltd wishes to thank the following for permission to reproduce the
paintings or photographs in their possession.

Barnaby's Picture Library for: Sir Robert Walpole; Duke of Newcastle; George Grenville; William Pitt the
Elder; Henry Addington.

Government Art Collection for: Duke of Devonshire; Duke of Portland; Sir Henry Campbell-Bannerman.

Hulton Deutsch Collection Ltd for: Spencer Compton; Henry Pelham; Marquess of Rockingham; Duke
of Grafton; Lord North; William Pitt the Younger; Lord Grenville; Earl of Liverpool; George Canning;
Viscount Goderich; Duke of Wellington; Earl Grey; Viscount Melbourne; Sir Robert Peel; Lord John
Russell; Earl of Derby; Earl of Aberdeen; Viscount Palmerston; Benjamin Disraeli; William Gladstone;
Marquess of Salisbury; Earl of Rosebery; Arthur Balfour; Herbert Asquith; David Lloyd-George; Andrew
Bonar Law; Stanley Baldwin; Ramsay MacDonald; Neville Chamberlain; Clement Attlee; Sir Anthony
Eden; Harold Macmillan.

National Portrait Gallery for: Earl of Bute; Earl of Shelburne; Spencer Perceval; Sir Winston Churchill.

Contents

Dod's Parliamentary Companion

Published annually since 1832

Dod's Parliamentary Companion is the United Kingdom's most authoritative political reference book. Over 1000 pages of fully updated facts about Peers, MPs and UK MEPs including their photographs and Political Interests. *Dod* publishes information about Government and leading organisations; Parliamentary Legislation, Ministerial Responsibilities and Select Committees. *Dod's Parliamentary Companion* is essential for effective communication with Government, the Civil Service and the European Community.

Dod's Parliamentary Companion,
PO Box 3700, Westminster, London SW1E 5NP
Telephone: 071 828 7256 Fax: 071 828 7269

Introduction

The Earl of Clarendon, recalling a suggestion in 1660 or 1661 that he give up the Lord Chancellorship and devote himself entirely to advising the King, condemned the notion of a 'first minister', 'a title so newly translated out of French into English, that it was not enough understood to be liked, and every man would detest it for the burden it was attended with'. Clarendon's comment nodded in the direction of the power exercised by Cardinals Richelieu and Mazarin in France, but did not acknowledge that similar roles had been played in England – by, for example, the Duke of Buckingham under James I and Charles I. A Prime Minister, in fact, was not obviously any different to a royal favourite, and attracted the same suspicion from those of the monarch's 'natural' counsellors – the nobility – that a favourite would have done. The belief that the position was an alien and sinister one persisted a long time: in 1741 Walpole's rule was condemned because 'a sole, or even a first minister is an officer unknown to the law of Britain, inconsistent with the constitution of this country, and destructive of liberty in any government whatsoever'.

The term became a fairly common one over the eighty years which separated the Restoration and the fall of Walpole, but its use remained unspecific, referring simply to a leading figure or figures within the government – although more often than not, it was the Lord Treasurer who was so identified. The Treasury's role in supplying the finance for the day-to-day expenses of government as well as its command of the money and the patronage which were used, with increasing sophistication, to confirm the loyalty of impecunious Members of Parliament made it naturally the centre of government, and its head naturally the leader of an administration. Walpole, first Lord of a Treasury which had been placed in commission, was little different in all this to his predecessors, save that he exercised his predominance from the House of Commons, and that he exercised it for so long. After Walpole, the association between the Prime Ministership and the head of the Treasury became customary, though not necessary: the elder Pitt never held the Treasury, although he was generally regarded as Prime Minister; nor did the Marquess of Salisbury, right at the end of the nineteenth century. In fact, as the association between the occupation of the Treasury and the premiership became formalised in the mid-eighteenth century, it had a slight tendency to lose its significance: first Lords such as Devonshire, Grafton, Rockingham or Portland were (at least for some of the time) little more than figurehead leaders of ministries carefully constructed out of a bewildering collection of political factions and family followings. Almost all eighteenth-century administrations were in fact coalitions of one kind or another, and their premiers only occasionally had more than a tenuous command over a diverse cabinet whose members were frequently either bitterly ignorant or scarcely aware of the policies being pursued by some of their colleagues.

Eighteenth-century Ministers were as much the personal servants of the Crown as had been their seventeenth-century predecessors and could be appointed and dismissed at will; yet the Crown's power to do so was increasingly tempered by the now obvious impracticability of a ministry which lacked the support of the House of Commons. The conflict between the King's right to appoint administrations and the Commons' ability to make their life impossible was a theme running through eighteenth-century politics. Even King William IV and Queen Victoria tried to retain ministries which were unable to guarantee Commons majorities.

By the end of the eighteenth century the Premiership had found its place as a regular part of the British constitution. But it was still regarded with sufficient distaste for a formal acknowledgement of the position to be slow in coming. Not until 1878 was it used officially, not until 1905 was the Prime Minister formally accorded precedence. The greater solidity of party and the elaboration of party machinery in the nineteenth century helped to give the premier a greater dominance within the government: the assumption of collective cabinet responsibility remained a rather vague doctrine in theory, but became considerably more influential in practice. The monarch's power to pick and choose her ministers ebbed away. Walter Bagehot described in 1867 the process by which a Prime Minister was made:

> As a rule, the nominal Prime Minister is chosen by the legislature, and the real Prime Minister for most purposes – the leader of the House of Commons – almost without exception is so. There is

nearly always some one man plainly selected by the voice of the predominant party in the predominant house of the legislature to head that party, and consequently to rule the nation. We have in England an elective first magistrate as truly as the Americans have an elective first magistrate.

Bagehot hinted at the growing tendency for governments to be dominated by their effective leader. Gladstone's famous Midlothian campaign of 1879-80 illustrated the way that the public perception of a government – or a potential government – become focussed on its leader (although Gladstone was in fact not formally the Liberal leader at the time). Prime Ministers of the present century have varied enormously in their approach to cabinet and the extent to which they have responded to discussion in cabinet or led it. The creation of a personal prime ministerial secretariat by Lloyd George during the First World War (his so-called 'Garden Suburb', housed in huts in the gardens of 10, Downing Street) appeared to indicate a determination to move beyond the mere chairmanship exercised by his predecessors, and a number of leaderships since then have provoked debate about a putative trend away from 'prime ministerial' and towards 'presidential' styles of government. But a Prime Minister's authority within the cabinet has always depended on political circumstance and a range of intangible factors: his indispensability to the party, his political skill, and the unity of his colleagues.

Dod's Parliamentary Companion Ltd wishes to acknowledge the help and advice of Paul Seaward in the compilation of this work.

Sir Robert Walpole
1676 – 1745

Sir Robert Walpole was born in 1676, the fifth child of Robert Walpole, a whig member of parliament in the Convention of 1689. He was educated at Eton and King's College, Cambridge. Through the death of his elder brothers in 1690 and 1698 he became heir to the estate, and abandoned a career in the Church, for which his father had intended him. In 1701 he was returned to parliament for Castle Rising, and in 1702 for King's Lynn, a seat he held until his ennoblement forty years later. The patronage of Sarah Churchill, later Duchess of Marlborough, brought him into contact with the leaders of the court whigs. When they came to power in 1708, Walpole became secretary at war; he was the government's factotum, the channel of communication between the Queen and the Duke of Marlborough, campaigning on the continent, and he was manager of the House of Commons. As Robert Harley and the Tories regained their influence with the Queen, the Whigs were squeezed out of government. Walpole survived longer than most; but in the wake of the Tory victory at the polls, in October 1711 he was dismissed.

Walpole found himself the most influential of the opposition Whig leaders in the Commons. In the bitter atmosphere caused by the debate over making peace with France, he was accused of venality and corruption in his conduct as Treasurer of the Navy. The Tory-dominated House voted him guilty, expelled him and committed him to the Tower of London. His expulsion became something of a *cause célèbre,* as his constituency insisted twice on re-electing him in spite of it. He was eventually released from the Tower in July 1712 and allowed to take his place in the Commons after the 1713 election.

When George I succeeded Anne in 1714, so the Whigs swept the Tories out of positions of power. Walpole became a Privy Counsellor and Paymaster of the Forces, in the government led by his brother-in-law, Lord Townshend, and in October 1715 he was appointed first lord of the Treasury and Chancellor of the Exchequer, marking his prominence in the ministry in a year in which he had been preoccupied with the defence of the Protestant settlement from the Jacobite threat. As Chancellor, Walpole devised the 'sinking fund', a scheme to reduce the enormous national debt left over from the war with France. The primacy of Townshend and Walpole was still threatened by a struggle for the Whig leadership with James Stanhope and the Earl of Sunderland, and complicated by friction with the King over foreign policy. In April 1717, Townshend was dismissed, and Walpole then resigned, as a result of their refusal to support the King's demands for hostile moves against Sweden in the wake of the discovery of a Jacobite plot involving the Swedish minister in London, Gyllenborg. In opposition, Walpole exploited his considerable nuisance value to the full, aggressively and often cynically attacking his former colleagues in government, and allying with the Tories and the Prince of Wales to do so.

The King was forced in early 1720 to bring Walpole and Townshend back into government in order to regain control over the Commons. But his return to power was secured by the South Sea Bubble. An attempt in 1720 to convert part of the national debt into South Sea Company stock resulted in speculative fever as investors pushed the price of the stock way above its realistic value. The inevitable crash came in September. Walpole had not been above investing in the scheme himself; nor had he foreseen its collapse (he lost some money); but his prescience seemed proven by his original opposition to major features of it, and his indispensability by the fact that no other member of the government was sufficiently distanced from it to resolve the problem. The actions he took provided little comfort for the many ruined by the crash, but ultimately contributed to the restoration of public credit, while his success in screening the government from the public outcry thoroughly restored him to the confidence of the King. Stanhope resigned, and Sunderland was dismissed. Townshend replaced the former as Secretary of State; Walpole was again appointed Chancellor of the Exchequer and First Lord of the Treasury. Sunderland's death in 1722 removed the last obstacle to the unchallenged ascendancy of what Walpole called 'the firm of Townshend and Walpole'.

Leaving foreign affairs to Townshend, Walpole reigned supreme in home affairs. He held sway in parliament by his deployment of the government's patronage to create a large court party, and also by his recognition of backbenchers' demand for stability, prosperity and low taxes. But his possession of power depended much on the confidence of the King, which Walpole assiduously cultivated. He dealt with opposition by stigmatising it as Jacobite, skillfully exploiting the plot of Bishop Atterbury in 1722. Opposition to Walpole, led by his former Whig colleague William Pulteney and the Tory Viscount Bolingbroke was lively (particularly in the journal *The Craftsman*), but largely ineffective. The most serious threats to the prime minister came from inside his government: the intrigues of Lord Carteret, the other Secretary of State, the Duke of Roxburgh, Secretary for Scotland, and the Earl of Macclesfield, the Lord Chancellor. Walpole deftly got rid of the first by moving him to Ireland; of the second by persuading the king that he had encouraged riots in Scotland against the new malt tax; and of the third by encouraging his impeachment for corruption. Less easily disposed of was the division which opened up between Walpole and Townshend themselves over the Treaty of Hanover in 1725, Townshend's attempt to isolate the Holy Roman Empire;

Walpole, haunted by the threat of an Imperial-Spanish alliance, began himself to dabble in foreign policy.

Walpole even managed the transition from one King to another with only a moment's pause. On George I's sudden death in June 1727 he fully expected to be replaced: George II disliked him and made it clear that he was unlikely to be asked to form a government. However, the failure of Spencer Compton to seize his opportunity, Walpole's offer to secure an increase in the civil list, and the influence of France brought George round: less than two weeks after the old king's death, Walpole and Townshend were reappointed. The late 1720s marked the highwater mark of Walpole's career. By now fabulously rich, he had almost completed his monumental house at Houghton, in Norfolk, and was building the finest picture collection in the country.

Walpole's power began slowly to crumble as Townshend and he moved further apart after the death of Townshend's wife, Walpole's sister, in 1726. In 1730 Townshend finally resigned. His departure strengthened the opposition, whose efforts at last bore fruit in the defeat of the excise scheme of 1733. Presented by the opposition as the first step towards extending the hated excise to cover food and clothing, an extraordinary public outcry was raised against it which forced the government to withdraw the proposal. Walpole's power had been seriously shaken for the first time. His troubles continued to gather. The Porteous riots in Edinburgh in 1736 were used to embarrass the government and divide its Scottish supporters; and in 1737 the King's quarrel with his son, Frederick, Prince of Wales, resulted in the creation of a new focus of opposition to the government and complicated Walpole's relations with George II.

It was events abroad, however, which were to lead eventually to Walpole's removal. Since Townshend had left, Walpole took the government's foreign relations upon himself. Determined to avoid military involvement abroad, in 1733 he had deflected the pressure to back the Imperial candidate to the throne of Poland against French intervention, promoting mediation instead. But the pressure for war with Spain as a result of Spanish interference with the (largely illicit) British trade with the Spanish colonies was more difficult to overcome – particularly when Captain Jenkins displayed in the Commons in 1738 his ear, cut off, so he said, by the Spanish coastguards. Walpole was reluctantly forced to declare war in October 1739, and shortly afterwards it embroiled him in the war of the Austrian Succession in support of Maria Theresa. His fortunes were by now well into decline. His majorities in the House were sinking, he was ill, and his advocacy of peace had left him deeply unpopular. Unrest in the country followed a severe winter and bad harvest in 1740. One of his closest allies, the Duke of Argyll, abandoned him for the opposition. The King's treaty with France which pledged Hanoverian neutrality in the coming war was much resented, and the odium of it unfairly cast upon Walpole.

Walpole held on through the disarray of the opposition, but in the general election of 1741 Walpole found his support slipping away. When the new parliament met, the government and its opponents were almost balanced; but as the process of hearing appeals against election decisions began, it became clear that the government's slim majority would be quickly worn away. By the beginning of February 1742, Walpole had recognised the inevitable and resigned.

He was created Earl of Orford and promised a pension; those of his government who survived his fall prevented the threatened full inquiry into his administration, and Walpole continued to advise the king informally, and exercise his influence over his party. He had not ruled out a return to power: by 1743, however, he was very ill, and in March 1745 he died.

Walpole married first in 1700 Catherine Shorter, the daughter of a Baltic timber merchant of Kent. The two were soon estranged and lived largely apart up to her death in 1737. He married in 1738 his mistress of some years, Maria Skerett, the daughter of an Irish merchant living in London: she died the year of their marriage, following a miscarriage. Unkempt and coarse, Walpole looked what he was, a Norfolk squire. For his opponents his lack of refinement stood for the whole grubby atmosphere of Whig politics. But Walpole's provincial manner disguised the shrewdest of political operators.

Spencer Compton
1673 – 1743

Spencer Compton was born in 1673, the third son of the third Earl of Northampton. He was educated at Trinity College, Oxford. Compton abandoned his family's long held Toryism, and switched his allegiance to the Whigs. In 1698 he was elected at Eye, Suffolk; his election to the chair of the Committee of Privileges and Elections in 1705 was a notable victory for the Whigs; but together with a number of colleagues, as one of the so-called 'Lord Treasurer's Whigs' he distanced himself from the opposition to the 'Junto' Whigs and supported the government, becoming as a result Treasurer and Paymaster of the Pensions. In the Tory General Election of 1710, he was defeated at Eye, but in 1713 secured election at East Grinstead, and in the election of 1714 he took the county (Sussex) seat. In the new Parliament he was elected speaker. His support for the Prince of Wales (whose treasurer he became) and his association with the circle of opposition politicians made the government contemplate removing him to the Lords in 1717. But Compton survived, and retained the Speakership in the Parliament of 1722, while also holding the office of Paymaster General.

Compton's moment appeared to have arrived in 1727, with the death of George I. The new king's hatred for Walpole prompted him apparently to turn to Compton to lead his government. Flustered, inexperienced, and, essentially rather incompetent, he turned to Walpole to help him with the details of preparing for the first meeting of the Privy Council. Whether Compton's failure to press his advantage was the reason for Walpole's success in regaining the initiative, or whether the King had never really intended Compton to be Prime Minister is unclear, but Walpole was soon confirmed in his old position. To compensate, Compton was created Baron Wilmington. In 1730 Walpole made him Lord Privy Seal, and advanced him to an earldom; later the same year he moved to become Lord President of the Council.

Wilmington's hapless failure in 1727 made him appear ridiculous; his acceptance of lesser prizes made him seem contemptible. But Wilmington's ambitions were not yet dead. Towards the end of Walpole's ministry he was actively intriguing against him, joining in the clamour for war with Spain, and in 1741 he abstained in the vote in the Lords on a motion for Walpole's removal. Walpole's resignation in February 1742 was followed immediately by a huge squabble over place and power between the factions which had engineered it. Wilmington's appointment as First Lord of the Treasury formed part of the strategy by which Walpole and the King intended to prevent Walpole's main opponents – Lord Carteret and William Pulteney – from succeeding to the position of dominance which he had relinquished. Carteret became Secretary of State, Pulteney was deftly manoeuvred into the Lords and out of any significant office whatsoever, and Walpole's seat was kept warm for his protégé, Henry Pelham. There was one flaw in the plot, for Carteret quickly established a rapport with the King through his willingness to indulge him in his anxious care for the defence of his Hanoverian possessions, which matured over the next year into a struggle over Hanover between Pelham, and Carteret and the King.

Wilmington himself was little more than a spectator of these intrigues. Horace

Walpole poisonously sketched him at the time: 'his only pleasure money and eating; his only knowledge forms and precedents; his only insinuations bows and smiles'. His death, unmarried, in July 1743, brought forward the struggle which eventually resulted in Pelham's triumph and Carteret's dismissal.

Henry Pelham
1695 – 1754

Henry Pelham was born in 1695, the younger son of the first Lord Pelham and his wife, Lady Grace Holles, the sister of John Holles, Duke of Newcastle. He was educated at Westminster School and at Hart Hall, Oxford. After service in the army, he was elected in 1717 for Seaford; in 1722 he took the Sussex seat, which he represented for the rest of his life. A follower of Townshend and Walpole, in 1721 he was appointed one of the Lords of the Treasury, in 1724 Secretary at War, and in 1730 Paymaster of the Forces. The support of his brother, the Duke of Newcastle, who disposed of a large number of parliamentary seats, was crucial to the survival of the Walpole regime: Pelham's principal role was to smooth the sometimes awkward relationship of the two.

Groomed by Walpole to succeed him, Pelham was 'more personally beloved by him than any man in England' (his rival, Lord Carteret, called him Walpole's 'chief clerk'). The factional politics surrounding Walpole's downfall, however, blocked Pelham's succession. The nonentity, Wilmington, went to the Treasury; Carteret dominated the new administration as Secretary of State. Pelham refused to accept the Chancellorship, although he acted as the government's leader in the Commons. But Pelham's command of the lower House made his title to succeed Wilmington after his death in August 1743 almost incontrovertible. He became first Lord of the Treasury.

It was some time before his dominance was established. Pelham and his brother, Newcastle (made the other Secretary of State) clashed with Carteret over the King's unpopular attempts to protect his small state of Hanover from becoming involved in the war of Austrian Succession while British troops fought in Germany on his behalf. Pelham, the heir to the Walpole doctrine of *quieta non movere,* and also the man responsible for persuading the House of Commons to stump up the money for the war, constantly resisted the expensive continental involvements which Carteret, without consulting the Pelhams, tried to take on. In November 1744, the Pelham brothers forced Carteret (now Earl Granville) to resign. The ministry was reorganised as a 'Broad Bottom' one, bringing in a number of Whig grandees and a couple of Tories (including Sir John Hynde-Cotton whose bulk made 'Broad Bottom' into a popular *double entendre*). The following year was an unhappy one: defeats on the continent were followed by the alarming, though unsuccessful, rebellion of the Jacobite pretender. The King's patent lack of confidence in his government, and his continued reliance on Granville and Lord Bath prompted the farce of February 1746, when the ministry resigned en bloc, only to be reinstated when Granville failed to form an administration. As a consequence, Pelham was able to insist that the King give the government his full confidence, ceasing to consult with 'private counsels' 'behind the curtain', and that the talented young member and virulent critic of the interests of Hanover, William Pitt, be included in the administration.

Pelham's ascendancy in the cabinet was assured. Despite his humiliation, the King's confidence in him began to grow. Granville and his ally, William Pulteney, Earl of Bath, never formed an effective opposition, and while

Frederick, Prince of Wales, gathered the discontents around him, they found little support.

Pelham brought to an end a war which was turning alarmingly in France's direction, and having convincingly won an early general election in 1747 – the quietest of the century – he concluded peace at the Treaty of Aix-la-Chapelle in October 1748. The armed forces, and government expenditure, were cut deeply; the interest on the National debt was reduced; by 1752 the land tax could be halved. In a series of Acts between 1746 and 1748, the government tried to remove some of the causes of Jacobite influence in Scotland. There were few issues for politicians to unite on; and, with the death of the Prince of Wales in 1751, no leaders for them to unite around. 'It is more fashionable', wrote Horace Walpole, 'to go to church than to either House of Parliament'. The ministry's life was not entirely placid: there were constant arguments between the brothers, Pelham and Newcastle, and with the king's brother, the Duke of Cumberland, largely occasioned by petty personal rivalries, by Newcastle's touchy jealousy (at times he and his brother were barely on speaking terms) and by the King's inveterate delight in trouble-making. Nor was it unadventurous: major changes in the law included the calendar reform of 1751 and the 1753 bill to permit the naturalisation of individual Jews – which had to be repealed the following session of parliament as a result of an outburst of popular anti-semitism.

Pelham died in office in March 1754, of an illness said to have been brought on by one of his occasional bouts of over-eating. He had in 1726 married Lady Catherine Manners, the daughter of the duke of Rutland. She died in 1780. Horace Walpole, a friend and political ally, wrote that Pelham 'lived without abusing his power, and died poor', and his integrity was widely acknowledged. Pelham's ambition had been to 'have relieved this nation from the vast load of debt, it now labours under', and had made some progress towards that end; he had also largely restored the political stability which his mentor, Walpole, had created. On hearing the news of Pelham's death, George II was said to have remarked sadly 'I shall now have no more peace'.

The Duke of Newcastle
1693 – 1768

Thomas Pelham-Holles, Duke of Newcastle-upon-Tyne, was born in 1693, the elder son of Thomas, first Lord Pelham and his wife Lady Grace, the sister of John Holles, Duke of Newcastle. He was educated at Westminster School and at Clare Hall, Cambridge. In 1711 he succeeded to the estate of his uncle, the duke of Newcastle, whereupon he added his surname to his own; the following year he also succeeded his father. His support for the Hanoverian succession earnt him his dukedom. By marriage he became close to the Whig leaders: his own, in 1717, to Lady Henrietta, the daughter of the second Earl of Godolphin, led him to support Sunderland in the Whig schism of that year. In 1724, however, Walpole recruited him – and, more importantly, his large personal electoral interest – making him Secretary of State.

Newcastle made himself irreplaceable not just by his own parliamentary following, but also by his assiduity as the manager of the whole government patronage machine. But in the last years of Walpole's administration, Newcastle became something of a liability: he quarrelled with the Duke of Argyll, the government's principal supporter in Scotland, and pressed Walpole to declare war on Spain. Newcastle played an important role in arranging the formation of the Wilmington government after Walpole's resignation in 1742. He retained the Secretaryship through Wilmington's brief premiership and into that of his own brother, Henry Pelham. Between them, the brothers struggled against the King's wish to fight France while protecting his small continental possession, Hanover, from involvement, and against the attempts of Lord Carteret (the other Secretary of State) to draw Britain more deeply into continental alliances. The Pelhams disposed of Carteret in 1746, and as soon as possible ended the war; in the process, however, Newcastle's meddlesome and irascible personality made office intolerable for his colleagues, and soon he was even quarrelling with his brother. Pelham was unenthusiastic about Newcastle's attempts to ensure the Austrian succession, which ended in an expensive and embarrassing failure.

When Pelham died, in March 1754, Newcastle took his place as first Lord of the Treasury. There was no obvious candidate, however, to replace his brother as dominant figure in the government. The two leading figures in the House, Henry Fox and William Pitt, both expected to succeed to a, if not the, leading position in the ministry. Fox refused to serve while Newcastle insisted on retaining control of the government's patronage machine; Pitt's venomous anti-Hanoverianism had already almost ruled him out as far as the King was concerned. Unsatisfied, the two of them made life intolerable for the ministry's agents in the lower House. Fox was eventually persuaded into the cabinet in December 1754, although not until November 1755 did he formally take on the role of Leader in the Commons. Newcastle's faltering efforts to provide for the protection of Hanover against the increasingly likely renewal of war with France exacerbated the government's weakness. Pitt, finally removed from even his junior offices, was left free to tear into the ministry's Hanoverian treaties. With Newcastle's reluctant declaration of war, and the military disasters of early 1756 – Byng's failure to protect Minorca, and reverses in America and India – Newcastle completely lost control of the Commons. In October 1756, deserted by Fox, he tendered his resignation. In consolation, he accepted a second dukedom.

As a resolution of the crisis following the dismissal of Pitt in April 1757 and the resignation of Devonshire, Newcastle returned to office as the nominal head of a comprehensive Whig ministry which combined Pitt as Secretary of State and Fox as Paymaster-General. The relationship was an uneasy one: Newcastle's rôle as the grumbling head of a ministry whose successes were generally attributed to Pitt was awkward and uncomfortable. Pitt bullied him and interfered at the Treasury. At the death of George II in October 1760, Newcastle remained at the head of the ministry, and presided over the remarkably quiet general election of 1761; but George III's antagonism towards the old Whigs and his patronage of his favourite, Lord Bute, ended the ministry soon afterwards. Even a common antipathy towards Bute could not make Newcastle and Pitt work together effectively. Pitt resigned in October 1761 after the cabinet refused to back his plans for a pre-emptive attack on Spain (whose threat to intervene in the war was soon afterwards realised); Newcastle himself resigned in May 1762, over the King's refusal to subsidise Britain's continental allies for another year.

Newcastle's departure was followed after a little while by a dramatic and thorough demolition of his political following. Towards the end of 1762 his friends and dependants who failed to abandon him for the new regime of Lord Bute were dismissed in the so-called 'Massacre of the Pelhamite Innocents'. It was the end of Newcastle's influence and the end of the party built by Walpole, although it was not quite the end of Newcastle's political career: Lord Rockingham added him to his ministry of 1765 as Lord Privy Seal. Newcastle's famous maladroitness was cruelly sketched by the memorialists of the reign of George II, all his enemies. For Horace Walpole he was 'a Secretary of State without intelligence, a Duke without money, a man of infinite intrigue without secrecy or policy, and a Minister despised and hated by his master, by all parties and ministries without being turned out by any'. But Newcastle's application and perseverance, a willingness to undertake drudgery that no one else would do, made him an essential figure from the 1720s to the 1760s: his political longevity reflected his indispensability. He died in November 1768.

The Duke of Devonshire
1720 – 1764

William Cavendish, fourth Duke of Devonshire, was born in 1720, the eldest son of the third duke, one of Walpole's closest friends and supporters. From 1741 until he was summoned to the House of Lords in his father's barony of Cavendish in 1751, he sat (as Lord Hartington) in the Commons for Derbyshire, one of the mainstays of the Pelham regime. In 1751 he was appointed Master of the Horse. He acquired large Irish interests by his marriage in 1748 to Charlotte, Baroness Clifford, the heiress of the Earl of Burlington and Cork. The dynastic alliance had been a match arranged early in his childhood, an arrangement which provoked Hartington's romantically-inclined mother to leave her husband. It seemed, however, to suit him: Lady Mary Wortley Montagu thought he had 'so great a vocation for matrimony that I verily believe if it had not been established before this time, he would have had the glory of the invention'. When his wife died in 1754, he was inconsolable. His kinsman, the Duke of Newcastle, in 1755 appointed him Lord Treasurer, Lord Lieutenant and General-Governor of Ireland. The following year he succeeded his father as Duke of Devonshire.

Devonshire came to head a ministry on Newcastle's resignation at the end of 1756 because he could attract the loyalty of the old Whigs in both Houses while being acceptable to William Pitt, whose popularity in opposition to Newcastle had rendered him inexcludable, and because he was tolerable to the King, as a way of masking the presence in the government of Pitt, whom (largely on account of his anti-Hanoverianism) he loathed. Devonshire became first Lord of the Treasury; Pitt the Secretary of State. The ministry was, however, painfully weak. Devonshire was uncomfortable about an arrangement which was, in effect, only a disguised coercion of the King; George II himself so detested Pitt that he merely waited for an opportunity to dispose of him; and despite Pitt's appeal to the country gentlemen in the House of Commons, the government possessed no solid foundations there. Pitt's temporary unpopularity over his attempt to win clemency for Admiral Byng – condemned to death for his failure to save Minorca from capture by the French – provided the King with the opportunity to dismiss him in April 1757. The following month Devonshire relinquished the Treasury and became Lord Chamberlain.

Devonshire remained an influential figure, attending cabinet meetings regularly (and unusually, for a Chamberlain) and struggling to hold together the ministry of his kinsman, Newcastle, after the accession of George III. Devonshire himself resigned in November 1762, in the wake of Newcastle's departure: like other of the Old Whigs, his resignation was followed by the loss of his local offices. Devonshire's brief ministry had, in effect, been Pitt's; Horace Walpole had called him (in comparison to his partner) 'a baby politician'. But while Devonshire may have been one of the youngest, he was also one of the grandest of the Whig grandees, and the messy failure of his government belied his ability, his common sense and his straightforwardness. He died in 1764.

The Earl of Bute
1713 – 1792

John Stuart, third Earl of Bute, was born in Edinburgh in 1713, the son of the second Earl of Bute and Lady Anne Campbell, daughter of the first Duke of Argyll. He was educated at Eton. In 1737 he was elected to the House of Lords as one of the Scottish representative peers. He had neither the money nor much of an inclination to play a major role in politics; shy, intellectual and rather stiff-mannered, he preferred to spend his time on his Scottish estates botanising or discussing agriculture and architecture with Scottish antiquarians. In 1747, however, in London, he became friendly with the Prince and Princess of Wales. After the death of Prince Frederick he became the confidant of his widow (gossip inspired by his enemies suggested rather more) and unofficial tutor and mentor of her son, George, the new Prince of Wales. Bute's influence on Prince George was profound, and his tuition thorough; in political matters he was, however, both inexperienced and imbued with the clichéd revulsion for ministerial vice and political corruption and the demand for a powerful 'patriot King' which had been common in the circle of Prince Frederick in the 1740s.

On the accession of the Prince in 1760 as George III, Bute shot to prominence. In March 1761 he was appointed one of the Secretaries of State. His colleagues resented the king's reliance on him, and were appalled by his political naivety. His – and the King's – determination to put an end to the 'bloody and expensive war' with France ran directly counter to William Pitt's ambitions for a convincing victory. Pitt resigned in October, having failed to persuade the cabinet to make a pre-emptive strike against Spain, now threatening to ally with France. Newcastle followed in May 1762, and Bute succeeded him as first Lord of the Treasury. Despite his contempt for the oligarchical power of the Old Whigs, Bute's government was at first little changed from that of Newcastle; it was only later, after he persuaded Henry Fox to join him as leader of the House of Commons, and after the preliminaries of peace with France were completed, that the general removal from office of those of the old regime who had failed to make the transition to Bute – the 'Massacre of the Pelhamite Innocents' – was perpetrated. Bute saw it as his principal task to end the war. His treaty of February 1763 was seen – particularly by Pitt – as sacrificing British gains too cheaply, but outside London and some sections of the merchant community, it was regarded as honourable and acceptable.

Bute's meteoric rise to power, and his ruthless destruction of the power of the Old Whigs, left enormous resentment among those whom he displaced. His Scottishness attracted English snobbery and suspicion; his accession to the vast Wortley inheritance in 1761 (he had married Mary, the heiress of Edward Wortley Montagu in 1736) added jealousy as a motive for reviling him. His views damned him, in the eyes of Whig politicians, as one dedicated to expanding the influence of the Crown and destroying the constitutional settlement of 1688. Never an enthusiastic minister, Bute was horrified at the virulence of the political satire to which he was subjected (particularly from the pens of Charles Churchill and John Wilkes). He reluctantly mobilised a counter-attack, employing, among others, William Hogarth, but he became determined to relinquish office. The last straw was the vigorous campaign against the proposal for a tax on cider of 1763. As soon as the measure had passed through parliament in April, Bute resigned.

Bute's resignation failed to put an end to the storm against him. He tried to secure the succession of a compliant successor, George Grenville, and remained at court, still – the 'minister behind the curtain' or 'Mayor of the Palace' – constantly consulted by the King. Grenville finally insisted that Bute leave the court, which he did in September 1763. Although Whigs continued to complain of Bute's secret influence with the Crown, it is unlikely that he had much after 1765. He continued occasionally to attend parliament, gaining election as a representative peer again in 1768 and in 1774. Bute's political education had been too much in rather half-baked theory and too little in practice, and had ill-prepared him (and the King) for government. As Samuel Johnson (one of the beneficiaries of his extensive patronage) said to Boswell, 'that Lord Bute, though a very honourable man, a man who meant well, a man whose blood was full of prerogative, was a bookman, and thought the country could be governed by the influence of the Crown alone'. Bute died in 1792.

George Grenville
1712 – 1770

George Grenville was born in 1712, the second son of Richard Grenville, and his wife Hester, the sister of Viscount Cobham of Stowe, near Buckingham. He was educated at Eton and Christ Church, Oxford, and was called to the bar at the Inner Temple. Viscount Cobham virtually adopted his nephews after the death of their father in 1727, and they became his allies in the vendetta which he waged against Walpole following his dismissal from the government in 1733. Grenville was elected in 1741 for the family seat of Buckingham, and joined in the campaign as one of 'Cobham's cubs' or the 'boy patriots', along with his senior, William Pitt.

Brought into the government after the Pelhams' expulsion of the Earl of Granville in 1744 as part of the 'Broad Bottom' administration, Grenville became in 1747 one of the Lords of the Treasury, and Treasurer of the Navy. He remained overshadowed by Pitt; the two grew, formally at least, closer together with Pitt's marriage in 1754 to Grenville's sister. In 1755 Grenville was sacked from Newcastle's government when he joined in Pitt's condemnation of its conduct of the war. In 1756, in the Devonshire-Pitt government, he returned to the Treasurership of the Navy; he resigned when Pitt was dismissed; in 1757 he was back again as part of the Newcastle-Pitt administration. But despite the family and political alliances which bound them, Grenville was irked by his subordinate status to Pitt. Like his colleague, he had formed a connection with the circle of the Dowager Princess of Wales and Lord Bute in 1755; unlike Pitt he maintained it and strengthened it over the next few years.

The accession of George III brightened Grenville's prospects for an independent political existence. On Pitt's resignation in 1761 he remained in the ministry providing its leadership in the House of Commons. On the resignation of Newcastle, in May 1762, Bute appointed Grenville Secretary of State for the northern department. But he was handicapped in the Commons by Bute's failure to entrust him with the government's patronage machine; his opposition to Bute's treaty which ended the Seven Years' War, though sincere, may have been accompanied by a belief that he could force more power out of Bute as the price of his acquiescence and agreement to promote the treaty in the Commons. Grenville had made the mistake of believing that he was indispensable: Bute replaced him with Henry Fox and shunted him off to the Admiralty, to complain bitterly of his humiliation and the drastic cut in his salary. Despite this, on Bute's retirement in April 1763, he recommended Grenville to the King as his successor. Grenville was Bute's last resort: Fox had declined to serve, and Grenville was simply the least objectionable of the other candidates. Bute ensured that he was hemmed in by more acceptable ministers, and hung around Whitehall, offering advice to the King. In August 1763, Grenville revolted against the arrangement, insisting on the King's full confidence and the dismissal of Bute from the Royal counsels. George III tried to find an alternative government, but failed. Strengthened in Parliament by an alliance with the Duke of Bedford, Grenville was left more solidly in power.

Two domestic issues dominated Grenville's two-year ministry, both of which contained strong elements of farce. The first was the attempt to silence the scurrilous anti-government satire of John Wilkes and his North Briton newspaper. The arrest of Wilkes, a Member of Parliament, on a general warrant for libel, and his expulsion from the House of Commons redounded savagely on the ministry. The other was the Regency Bill of 1765, rendered necessary by the onset of George III's illness. Misunderstandings between the King and the Prime Minister concerning the choice of regent served to complete the alienation of the two. Of more long term significance was Grenville's solution to the growing financial burden of the defence of the colonies, vastly expanded after the gains of the war of 1756-63. The House of Commons agreed in February 1765 to a set of resolutions imposing on America the same stamp duties which were already in force in England, while other legislation imposed duties on some goods imported into America.

The Stamp Act was to produce an outcry in the colonies, but by the time it did, Grenville was out of office. His deteriorating relationship with the King made coexistence impossible: the two were constantly at odds over matters of patronage, and the King found Grenville's manner intolerable. 'I would rather', he said, 'see the devil in my closet than Mr Grenville'; 'every day', he complained to Bute, 'I meet with some insult from these people'. The King's search for an alternative was at first abortive, throwing him humiliatingly back on Grenville, but it finally bore fruit in the ministry created under the auspices of the King's uncle, the Duke of Cumberland, and headed by the Marquess of Rockingham. In July 1765 Grenville was dismissed.

In opposition, Grenville fought an intense battle against the Rockingham government's reversal of his stamp duties. The events of 1763-65 had left George III with a lasting aversion to Grenville which meant that he never again held office; and undoubtedly Grenville lacked any trace of charm. As his cousin, Thomas Pitt, said of him, 'he had nothing seducing in his manners... he was diffuse and argumentative, and never had done with a subject after he had convinced your judgment till he had wearied your attention'. But Grenville was nevertheless one of the most able and conscientious ministers of his time, attracting the admiration of Edmund Burke for his ambition 'to raise himself, not by the low, pimping politics of a court, but to win his way to power, through the laborious gradations of public service'. He died in November 1770.

The Marquess of Rockingham
1730 – 1782

Charles Watson-Wentworth, second Marquess of Rockingham, was born in 1730, the son of the first Marquess and his wife, Mary Finch, the daughter of the sixth Earl of Winchilsea and second Earl of Nottingham. He was educated at Westminster school and St John's College, Cambridge. He succeeded his father in 1751, and married in 1752 Mary Bright, a great Yorkshire heiress as well as a sensible, tactful and trusted political adviser. Rockingham was scarcely one of the brightest and best of a new generation of Whig grandees; but (as far as the strategists of the Old Whig party were concerned) he made up in wealth and electoral influence what he lacked in brain power. His uncle, William Murray (later Lord Chief Justice Mansfield) undertook, largely unsuccessfully, his political education.

Rockingham in fact took little interest in national politics until the assault on the power of the Whig party mounted by George III and Lord Bute. With the other Old Whigs, Rockingham was stripped of his offices at the end of 1762 in the 'Massacre of the Pelhamite Innocents'. With Newcastle, and the Dukes of Portland and Grafton, he became one of the leaders of the Whigs as they fought back. Their return to power came as a result of the final breakdown of relations between George III and George Grenville in the summer of 1765. The King commissioned his uncle, the Duke of Cumberland, to find an alternative government. The Whigs were left bemused by the refusal of William Pitt, the politician of the greatest stature, to take office; but Cumberland did, eventually, construct a new Whig ministry in July. Rockingham, to his own surprise, became nominal head of the government as first Lord of the Treasury; the old Duke of Newcastle became Lord Privy Seal; Grafton became one of the Secretaries of State. But Cumberland himself, although without an official position, was the dominant figure. It was a young (Rockingham was thirty-five) and inexperienced ministry, stuffed with aristocrats, but with little talent in the House of Commons; with the opposition of Bute's supporters and Pitt's attitude unclear, few expected it to last out the winter's session of Parliament. Its life seemed even shorter following Cumberland's death in October.

In the event, it did last for one gruelling parliamentary session. Grenville's legacy had included the unexpected storm of defiance in America to his Stamp Act. Rockingham, unusually susceptible to the appeal from commercial and manufacturing interests, was quickly convinced of the necessity of the Act's repeal. But although it repealed it, the government was forced by opinion on all sides of the political spectrum to couple with repeal a face-saving assertion of parliament's legislative supremacy over the colonies. Despite this gesture, the repeal was carried only with the support of Pitt, the backing of a brilliant campaign mounted in the Commons by Rockingham's able young secretary, Edmund Burke, and against the opposition of Grenville and the grumbles of the King. In any case, the doubts about the ministry's ability to survive persisted. The Duke of Grafton resigned in May 1766, complaining about the government's failure to draw in Pitt; Pitt himself began to make the ministry's vulnerability to his open opposition painfully obvious. Rockingham had come to office largely because the King could think of no-one else whom he could bear; by the summer of 1766 even Rockingham (who paid scant respect to his royal master) had come to seem no better than the other possibilities. In July 1766 the King dismissed the ministry, and asked Pitt to form a government. Rockingham's dismissal and its sequel in effect contributed to the birth of a new Whig party out of the ashes of the old. Pitt's determination to exclude Rockingham and his followers from a government to be 'formed of the best and ablest men, – without any regard to parties, distinctions, or connections' crystallised a split between two radically different conceptions of political priorities: Rockingham's dedication to the Old Whig tradition of party loyalty and resistance to royal power; Pitt's anti-party 'patriotism', close to the principles and prejudices with which George III had begun his reign. Rockingham and his followers drew out the implications of the split, most famously in Burke's *Thoughts on the Causes of the present discontents:* the real influence in government they attributed to Lord Bute, and the real aim of the government, they claimed, was the corruption of the House of Commons and the destruction of the constitution.

Despite the strength of their rhetoric, Rockingham and his followers proved ineffective in opposition, partly because Rockingham himself had little interest in the real exertion which it would have required, and partly because his, and his followers' elevation of consistency and party purity into a ruling principle left them unable to form a proper alliance with any other group, least of all with Pitt (now Earl of Chatham) with whom they nevertheless shared a deep opposition to the American war. The Rockinghams' demand for the reduction in the 'influence of the Crown' struck a chord in the 1770s, helping to spark the creation of regional reform movements, such as Christopher Wyvill's Yorkshire Association in Rockingham's own backyard; but Rockingham would not patronise a movement calling for electoral reform, which might destroy the power of Whig grandees such as himself, and the reforming initiative tended to pass to his rivals, the Chathamites.

The failure of the American war and the collapse of Lord North's government in 1782 brought Rockingham a final and brief return to office. There being little alternative, the King was forced to turn to the leaders of the opposition, and in March Rockingham became the nominal head of a ministry which combined his own followers and those of Chatham, now (since his death in 1778) led by the Earl of Shelburne. Rockingham became first Lord of the Treasury, Shelburne and Charles James Fox the two Secretaries of State. The new government reluctantly conceded to the growing Irish agitation measures of relief for Irish Catholics and for Ireland's legislative independence from Westminster; the interest in the reduction of the influence of the Crown produced a series of Acts abolishing a number of sinecures and obsolete offices; but with the Rockinghams and Chathamites united over the need to end the war, but unable to agree on whether that should entail cutting America loose, the ministry failed to secure peace. Rockingham died on 1 July, just as the coalition was splitting up over America, and the Rockingham Whigs were themselves divided over parliamentary reform.

Rockingham's two periods in office were brief, and his qualifications to lead the Whigs were doubtful – he was, wrote one contemporary, 'only known to the public by his passion for horse races'. But Rockingham presided over a marked change in the political and constitutional outlook of the Whig party. As articulated by Burke, Rockingham's leadership represented an acceptance (even a celebration) of the existence of party, condemned in the past as mere faction, and a new Whig identity, based on an opposition to the influence of the Crown.

William Pitt (the Elder)
1708 – 1778

William Pitt was born in 1708, the grandson of the rich India merchant and Governor of Madras, Thomas Pitt, and the second son of Robert Pitt of Boconnoc, Cornwall. William Pitt was educated at Eton and Trinity College, Oxford. His brother's marriage in 1731 drew him into the circle of Richard Temple, Viscount Cobham, whose patronage bought him an army commission. In 1735 he entered the House of Commons as member for the family borough of Old Sarum.

In the Commons Pitt made his mark as one of 'Cobham's Cubs', pursuing the old Viscount's vendetta against Walpole. Pitt's sarcastic speech in 1736 on George II's squabbles with his son, Frederick, Prince of Wales, earnt him the anger of the King and dismissal from the army. Pitt moved close to the opposition circle around the Prince at Leicester House, and joined in the campaign for war with Spain to which Walpole eventually succumbed. His opposition to the court did not (like the Prince's) end with Walpole's fall. He earnt popularity (and a large legacy from Sarah, the dowager Duchess of Marlborough) through his attacks on a foreign policy which seemed too closely linked to the interests of the King's little continental state of Hanover; for the King it only confirmed his dislike. After the Pelhams had jettisoned Earl Granville, the King's pro-Hanoverian supporter, in November 1744, Pitt and his Cobham allies saw the chance of an accession to power. Pitt's path to preferment was blocked, however, by the King until the fiasco of Granville's own attempt to form an administration in February 1746 permitted Pelham to insist on his being brought into the government as joint Vice-Treasurer of Ireland. In May he was advanced to be Paymaster-General of the Forces.

Pitt's appointment left his former friends disillusioned with his much-trumpeted 'patriotism', although he tried to maintain his popular reputation over the next seven years in office by ostentatiously refusing to take the job's famously valuable perquisites. In 1754 he strengthened his alliance with the Temple dynasty through marriage to Hester, the sister of George Grenville, another of Cobham's group; but his alliance with the Pelhams did not survive Henry Pelham's death in March 1754. Newcastle's failure to recognise his talents and particularly his rhetorical dominance in the House of Commons with a more senior appointment left him furious, exposing with vengeful pleasure the inadequacies of the government's leadership there; intriguing with a new Prince of Wales, the sixteen-year-old who was to become George III, Pitt attacked the feeble preparations which Newcastle had made for the looming war with France and his attempts to construct a series of continental alliances for the protection of Hanover from invasion. Pitt was dismissed from his post in November 1755, leaving him free to attract an enormous amount of public attention with his contemptuous condemnation of Newcastle's employment of German mercenaries to fight the coming war, and with his proposal for a popular, militia-based army.

The reverses of the first year of war left Newcastle's ministry crumbling; failing in his attempt to obtain Pitt's support, Newcastle resigned in November

1756. In spite of all the King could do to prevent it, Pitt, declaring that 'I know that I can save this country and no-one else can', was the only person who seemed able to inspire the confidence of the Commons. Pitt took office as Secretary of State for the southern department and Leader of the House of Commons in a ministry formally headed by the Duke of Devonshire. But despite his popularity, Pitt lacked the formal support in the Commons which Newcastle had enjoyed: the serried ranks of government placemen largely owed their positions to the Pelhams, and their loyalty was questionable. It was the King's attitude, however, which was most likely to bring about the ministry's premature end. Pitt did his best to placate him, but George II was bored by his 'long speeches, which might possibly be very fine, but were greatly beyond his comprehension', and anxious to get rid of a set of ministers whom he referred to as 'scoundrels'. Pitt's dismissal came in April 1757, when his popularity appeared to have diminished following his manifest reluctance to have Admiral Byng executed for his failure to defend Minorca against the French. In response, he organised a dramatic, country-wide campaign for his reinstatement: for a few weeks it was said to 'rain gold boxes' on the ousted minister. Not for six weeks was the crisis resolved: Newcastle and Pitt were reconciled, and Newcastle made formal leader of an administration in which Pitt, as Secretary of State, was again the real premier. With Pitt's prestige and Newcastle's parliamentary following, the ministry was impregnable.

Pitt took most of the credit for the remarkable British successes in the war from 1758 onwards. He had a hand in even the smallest details, while his energy and his rhetorical power captured the public imagination. By 1760 most of Canada had fallen to the British, France's navy had virtually been denied the sea, and her armies thoroughly beaten on the continent by Britain's German allies (whom Pitt had come, belatedly, to respect and value). Pitt had won extraordinary prestige. But George III's accession in 1760 spelt the end of his dominance. The new King and his friend and mentor, Lord Bute, had been allied with Pitt in the mid 1750s, but since Pitt's acceptance of office the relationship had cooled considerably. The King's determination to end the war, which was supported by Bute, was directly contrary to Pitt's ambition to gain the maximum advantage from it. The disagreements within the government grew as 1761 wore on, and came to a head as Spain agreed to throw its weight into the war on the side of France. Pitt's plans to strike a pre-emptive blow against Spain were opposed by Bute, and the rest of the cabinet, including Newcastle. Pitt rather petulantly resigned in October, although he accepted a barony for his wife and a pension as a token of the King's gratitude for his wartime services.

Never very well, Pitt was beginning to show signs of the mysterious debilitating mental illness which was to plague him at the end of the 1760s, and he spent the next years in semi-retirement. He emerged periodically, theatrically dragging himself from his bed of sickness to attack the terms of Bute's peace with France and Grenville's efforts to tax the American colonies. But despite his incapacity, Pitt remained the dominant figure in British politics. Courted by a series of feeble administrations, Pitt set such conditions on his participation in government that he joined none of them. Not until the collapse of Rockingham's government in July 1766 did he return to office, on his own terms, and clearly at the head of his own ministry, as the King finally recognised the impossibility of his exclusion. His acceptance of office led to a final split from the core of the Old Whig party of Lord Rockingham, with which he had long had an equivocal relationship. Enthusiastically he espoused the anti-party rhetoric of the King and Lord Bute, and declared that the government would be one of ability, regardless of connection or party. George III congratulated him on his ambition to restore 'that subordination to government, which can alone preserve that inestimable blessing, Liberty, from degenerating into licentiousness'. Pitt freed himself from the burden of departmental responsibility and the vexations of life in the Commons, breaking with tradition by leading the government as Lord Privy Seal and taking a peerage, as Earl of Chatham. The Duke of Grafton became first Lord of the Treasury.

Chatham's government was not the triumphant success which had been looked for from the vanquisher of France. His plans to create a network of continental alliances to prepare for the resumption of the rivalry met with indifference from the putative allies; his sympathy for the American colonists' resistance to taxation by the British Parliament was not enough to set their discontent to rest. His acceptance of office and a peerage did much to tarnish Chatham's popular reputation; it also exacerbated his illness. Chatham grew more irritable, developed eccentricities, and lost all powers of concentration. For much of the time, he felt unable to be in London. The government drifted, leaderless and largely policyless, until in early 1767 Grafton unwillingly assumed the responsibility. In order to strengthen the government, Grafton took in the followers of the Duke of Bedford. Bedford's hostility to Pitt, to his loyal ally, the Earl of Shelburne, and to their views on American policy finally provoked Chatham to resign in October 1768.

Chatham did recover, slowly, from his illness. In 1770 he returned to the Lords, and his blistering denunciation of the government's conduct – over the expulsion from the Commons of an old ally, John Wilkes, and over America – helped to bring about the fall of Grafton. He made a second comeback in 1774 in an attempt to avert the slide towards the American rebellion, cooperating with Benjamin Franklin, the agent of the American colonies. Chatham supported the struggle of the colonists against the assertion of Parliament's right to tax them, but he deprecated their assumption of independence. His last speech in the House of Lords was made in opposition to the proposal by the Rockinghamites to allow the Americans their freedom. Immediately afterwards he collapsed; a few weeks later, in April 1778, he died.

In the late 1750s and 1760s Pitt had towered above his colleagues and rivals. Always an isolated figure, he rejected one of the basic assumptions of eighteenth century politics – the dominance of aristocratic 'connection'. Pitt's 'patriotism', which described the abandonment of party interests for the more high-minded pursuit of national objectives by the most able ministers, was in fact a highly artful pose which was his most effective weapon in the struggle to secure place and power. Pitt was remembered, above all else, as a great war leader. Although the Seven Years War had been won by the combined efforts of a thousand talented, often brilliant, soldiers, sailors and administrators, it had been Pitt's enormous energy and determination which had driven them all on.

The Duke of Grafton
1735 – 1811

Augustus Henry Fitzroy, third Duke of Grafton was born in 1735, the grandson of the second Duke and a direct descendant of the illegitimate son of Charles II. He was educated at Westminster School and at Peterhouse, Cambridge. Elected to the House of Commons for Bury St Edmunds in 1756, the following year he succeeded his grandfather as Duke. Grafton was drawn into serious politics, like his near-contemporary the Marquess of Rockingham, by the assault on the power of the Whig grandees mounted by George III and Lord Bute in 1762-63; in the proscription of the Old Whigs which followed the resignation of the Duke of Newcastle, Grafton lost the Lord Lieutenancy of Suffolk. He formed a close association with Pitt, whom he came to regard with an exaggerated reverence and follow with excessive devotion. Grafton's distaste for public life, and his preference for the race track and his library quickly reasserted themselves. He joined Rockingham's administration as secretary of state for the northern department, but only on the understanding that it would soon gain the support and participation of Pitt. That failing, he resigned in May 1766. In July the same year Pitt did eventually agree to lead a ministry. His health failing, he declined the traditional post of first Lord of the Treasury, and the burden of overseeing his own department, and became instead Lord Privy Seal and went to the Lords as Earl of Chatham. Grafton, his most dedicated supporter, took the Treasury in his place.

At first, Grafton was nothing more than Chatham's cipher; but within a few months Chatham's mental illness rendered him incapable of leadership. Grafton was unwilling to take over, and the ministry drifted, leaderless and directionless. Opposed by a miscellany of discontents, its ability to control the Commons lay largely in the hands of the brilliant but erratic Charles Townshend. Grafton had finally accepted responsibility for leading the government mid-way through 1767, largely out of a sense of duty and loyalty to the King, as well as a growing frustration with Chatham. Townshend's unexpected death, in September 1767, removed one of the government's main props, and made a reconstruction of the ministry urgent. Grafton turned to the Duke of Bedford and his parliamentary following to provide the government with a reinforcement; but the Bedford alliance confirmed the gulf which had opened up between Grafton and his former patron, for Chatham and Bedford were personally hostile to one another and differed strongly on policy matters – among other things, Bedford added a hard edge to the government's policy on America. In October 1768 Chatham and his associate Shelburne resigned.

More securely seated in power, the Grafton ministry was as plagued as its predecessors had been by the dilemmas of America and the pain of John Wilkes's attempt to secure parliamentary immunity against conviction for blasphemy and seditious libel. Returning from continental exile, the popularity which his persecution of Bute had brought him secured Wilkes election at Middlesex in 1768. When the government nevertheless insisted on the execution of his sentence and began (rather contrary to Grafton's own instincts) moves to expel him from the Commons, Wilkes skillfully arranged a storm of popular protest.

Meanwhile, the government still attempted to follow Grenville in trying to enforce contributions from the colonies towards colonial defence. Townshend's attempt in 1767 to raise customs revenue from the colonies brought protests which culminated in the Boston massacre of 1770. The government backed down, repealing all the duties, save that on tea, a token of parliamentary sovereignty insisted on by Bedford and his supporters. The coalition of Wilkites and supporters of the colonists placed intense pressure on the government. Wilkes was expelled from the House of Commons in February 1769, but Middlesex returned him again and again: when the Commons at last simply imposed the losing candidate on the shire it provoked a wave of riots and demonstrations. Chatham returned to denounce the government in the Lords, and his remaining followers resigned from the administration. Insecurely in command of his cabinet, smarting from the nicely targeted satires of the mysterious 'Junius', Grafton's morale was not improved when his wife, Anne Liddell (whom he had married in 1756) finally left him for the Earl of Upper Ossory, following Grafton's own very public affair with Nancy Parsons, Mrs Hutton. He divorced her, and remarried in 1769, Elizabeth Wrottesley, the daughter of the Dean of Windsor and a relative of Bedford. But Grafton had had enough, and resigned in January 1770.

Grafton did take office again, as Lord Privy Seal, in Lord North's government in 1771, largely, he claimed, in an attempt to moderate its policy towards America. In 1775 he resigned. He was Privy Seal again in the ministries of Rockingham and Shelburne in 1782-3. In his later years, Grafton turned pious, became a unitarian, and wrote a number of pamphlets on liturgical revision. He died in 1811.

Lord North
1732 – 1792

Frederick, Lord North, was born in 1732 into a prominent Tory family. His father, the first Earl of Guilford, was an associate of Frederick, Prince of Wales (who was North's godfather), and one of the tutors of his son, the future George III. North was brought up close to the young Prince George. Educated at Eton and Trinity College, Oxford, in 1754 he was returned at the General Election for the family seat of Banbury. In 1756 he married Anne Speke, a Somerset heiress. Despite his Tory leanings, North owed his first government office, as one of the Lords of the Treasury, to his kinship with the Whig grandee, the Duke of Newcastle. In 1766 Chatham made him Joint Paymaster of the Forces, and North's patent ability and popularity ensured that on the death of Charles Townshend in September 1767, he replaced him as Chancellor of the Exchequer and as the ministry's leading spokesman in the Commons. As such, he was responsible for the duel between the House and the electors of Middlesex over the expulsion of John Wilkes; he was also the principal advocate within the cabinet for the retention of the duty on tea out of the import duties which Townshend had imposed on the American colonies – a decision, intended to mark Parliament's right to tax the colonies, which crystallised the points at issue in the long running dispute and which led ultimately to war in 1775.

On Grafton's resignation, the King was happy to find in Lord North, at last, an obvious successor as premier who was highly acceptable to himself. North might have been forgiven for being less happy, with George Grenville, Lord Rockingham, the Earl of Chatham and even the Duke of Grafton ranged in opposition to him. Within months, however, North had established his authority over the Commons, and within a few years, he had banished the febrile factional politics of the 1760s. With a reaction against the extremism of Wilkes's campaign setting in, North was able to tap a reservoir of backbench loyalism; the opposition factions, riven by their furious struggle for power over the last few years, remained unable to cooperate effectively. Although the attacks of the Rockinghamite Whigs on the secret influence of the Crown added to the pressure for parliamentary and ministerial reform which had built up as a result of the Wilkes affair, the impetus of the affair itself was largely spent. Wilkes, indeed, paled into insignificance against the unfolding crisis in America.

North had pronounced the dispute with the colonists settled in 1771; but it had in fact barely begun. The reduction in the duties on British tea imported into the colonies in 1773 as part of the settlement of the financial affairs of the bankrupt East India Company, began a chain of events leading to the War of Independence. Resentment at the preferential treatment for British tea contributed to the reviving discontent in America, and resulted in the Boston 'tea party' of December 1773. Responding to a popular demand in Britain for an effective response, in 1774 North introduced a series of retaliatory measures amounting to government control over the Massachusetts Bay colony. Meanwhile, the solution to the problem of governing the French Roman Catholic population in Canada, the Quebec Act of 1774, exacerbated the colonists' fears of arbitrary rule and added to them the fear of popery.

North's convincing win in general election of September 1774 helped to propel him, though reluctantly, into confrontation with the colonies. His unpopular attempt at conciliation in February 1775 came too late. By April British forces had clashed with the rebel militia, and the rebellion soon turned into a wider conflict: France joined in in February 1778, Spain a year later. The colonists' struggle, and the cost of combating it, stimulated political unrest closer to home: in Ireland, a demand for free trade with the British colonies (granted in 1780) and for the removal of the legislative supremacy of the British Parliament; in England, the movement for reform of parliament and government revived. North had offered his resignation to the king following the humiliating defeat at Saratoga in 1777, but it had been refused. Over the next three years, North regularly begged the King to release him, pleading his inadequacy for the job of wartime leader. Affairs of state, he told the King in 1778, 'can hardly be well conducted unless there is a person in the Cabinet capable of leading, of discerning between opinions, of deciding quickly and confidently, and of connecting all the operations of government, that this nation may act uniformly and with force. Lord North is not such a man'. In 1780 the Gordon riots in London and the defection of the old Bedford connection from the government added to North's misery – although in the election of that year, concern at the success and radicalism of the reform movement helped him to retain his majority.

North regarded the defeat at Yorktown in October 1781 as conclusive, but the King insisted on carrying on the struggle, against the mood both of the public and the House of Commons. North's strength in the Commons, which had rested for so long on the approval of the mass of backbench members, began to waste away. By February 1782, North could no longer guarantee the support of the House for continued operations in America and resigned. George III felt personally betrayed; his former fondness for North was replaced by bitterness.

The rejection in parliament of the peace treaty negotiated by Shelburne brought North back into power. To the King's disgust, the only combination which could command support in the Commons was one of North and Charles James Fox, the leading follower of the late Lord Rockingham in the Commons, whose part in the debauching of the Prince of Wales had earnt him the King's lasting hostility. He had little choice but to accept it, however, and in March 1783 the new coalition took office, under the nominal leadership of the Duke of Portland, who had inherited the overall leadership of Rockingham's party following his death the previous July. Fox and North were united only by their opposition to the Treaty, but the combination proved remarkably workable. The ministry was strangled, however, not long after its birth, by the King. Fox's attempt to take the affairs of the East India Company under parliamentary control provided his opportunity. Aided by the young William Pitt, he secured the rejection of the Bill in the Lords, and dismissed the government.

The rise of Pitt as the King's new favourite sent North into the political wilderness. Much of the support he had built up in the 1770s defected to Pitt or else was turned out in the election of 1784. North succeeded his father as Earl of Guilford in 1790, and he died two years later. 'It is a paltry eulogium for the Prime Minister of a great country', Horace Walpole remarked, 'yet the best that can be allotted to Lord North is that though his country was ruined under his administration, he preserved his good humour'. Walpole was never particularly fair-minded. North had occupied office as Britain suffered its first, and only, major military defeat of the century, and the taint of it proved impossible to remove, for all that the war, after the entry of France and Spain, was impossible to win. North recognised that early on; his royal master had not.

The Earl of Shelburne
1737 – 1805

William Petty, second Earl of Shelburne, was born in Dublin in 1737, the elder son of the first Earl of Shelburne, who had come, quite late in life, to inherit the great Petty fortune. Thereafter, his parents devoted their energies to taking fashionable London society by storm (though their provincial manners and his mother's ambition made them rather comic figures) and they neglected him. Shelburne went up to Christ Church, Oxford, and served in the army; he ended his military career in 1760 as a Colonel and as Aide-De-Camp to the King. He was elected to Parliament in 1760, for the Petty family borough of Chipping Wycombe; in 1761 he succeeded his father, sitting in the English House of Lords in his father's English title of Baron Wycombe, although he was generally known under the Irish title, Shelburne.

Shelburne had become a clever, well-read intellectual. His Irish background, however, left him something of an outsider in the clannish world of Whig politics, and his attempts to overcome his isolation with an ingratiating manner only made it worse. His early adherence to Lord Bute cut him out of the circle of the Old Whigs. He took office (at Bute's insistence, but without Grenville's enthusiasm) in Grenville's government, as President of the Board of Trade. But Shelburne had found a more inspiring mentor in William Pitt – a figure almost as isolated as he was himself. Shelburne resigned in 1763, following Bute's failure to lever Grenville out of office to make way for Pitt. The two became politically very close, though personally (to Shelburne's annoyance) still distant. With Pitt, Shelburne condemned Grenville's Stamp Act, and the notorious general warrant used to arrest John Wilkes. His defence of Wilkes incurred the King's displeasure and the loss of his military office.

Shelburne received his reward on the formation of the Pitt-Grafton government, in 1766, becoming Secretary of State for the southern department. Close to the commercial interests of the City of London (he was a shareholder in the East India Company), he struggled to find a means to conciliate the Americans. But as Chatham declined into mental illness, his efforts were undermined by other members of the cabinet, particularly by the taxation proposals of the Chancellor, Charles Townshend. Shelburne became increasingly isolated as the last voice of Chathamite policies left in the government. In December 1767 Grafton brought into the ministry the Duke of Bedford and his friends; the responsibility for the colonies was taken away from Shelburne and given to Lord Hillsborough, an associate of Lord North. In October 1768 Shelburne and Chatham resigned.

Shelburne's support for Wilkes and his opposition to Wilkes's expulsion from the House of Commons put him into contact with London radical and dissenting circles, and he began to become associated with the movement for the reform of government and Parliament. With the death of Chatham in May 1778, Shelburne succeeded to the leadership of his small group of personal followers. In uneasy alliance with the Rockingham Whigs, Shelburne kept up the attack on a government weakened by the disasters of the American war. When North's government finally collapsed, Shelburne, despite his radical tendencies and his opposition to the war, was fixed on by the King as one leader who would at least not try, or be able to bully him; for Shelburne had, as much as Chatham, rejected party as the guiding principle of politics, and, also like Chatham, had made much of his respect for the prerogative of the Crown. A ministry would not have been viable, however, without the parliamentary strength provided by the Rockinghams, and Shelburne accepted office in March 1782 as Home Secretary in a ministry formally led by Rockingham. The alliance remained an uneasy one. The Rockinghams were willing to cut ties with America; Shelburne, like Chatham, was firmly opposed to a final break. Despite a common interest in government reform, Shelburne and the Rockinghamites failed to collaborate on proposals for 'economical reform'. Charles James Fox, the Rockinghamite Foreign Secretary, and Shelburne particularly disliked and distrusted one another. Shelburne, indeed, was cordially despised by almost everyone. When Rockingham died, on 1 July, the alliance fell apart. The King appointed Shelburne to succeed him, in preference to the Duke of Portland, Rockingham's political heir. Fox led the Rockinghamites, en bloc, out of the government.

The support of the King was no substitute for the solid parliamentary backing which the Rockinghamite Whigs had provided. Lacking any real strength, Shelburne's ministry only survived as long as it did because Parliament was in recess for most of its short life. Its main, and most urgent task was the settlement of peace. Reluctantly conceding independence to the American colonies, while hoping to maintain at least a fraternal relationship with them, Shelburne was regarded as having struck a rather feeble deal – failing in particular to secure any commitment to compensation for victimised American loyalists. As soon as Parliament returned, it was obvious that Shelburne and his peace treaty were doomed. The address approving the peace was defeated by a coalition of Fox and Lord North and their followers in February 1783. At the end of the month Shelburne resigned, to the annoyance of the King, thus forced to accept his least favourite politician, the rake and *bon viveur* Charles James Fox.

Shelburne's career petered out. The young William Pitt was now ready to inherit the mantle of his father and the leadership of the small Chathamite following. He made Shelburne Marquess of Lansdowne in 1785. Lansdowne drifted away from his radical interests of the 1770s, although he backed the resistance to the repressive measures employed by Pitt in the 1790s to meet the dangers of sedition in the wake of the French Revolution. His support for parliamentary reform declined, and his mind turned to more theoretical concerns, as he cultivated the continental *philosophes* and philosophic radicals such as Jeremy Bentham. Even they appeared to dislike him, though they accepted his patronage. Bentham cattily remarked that he had 'talked his vague generalities in the House of Lords in a very emphatic way, as if something grand were at the bottom of it all, when, in fact, there was nothing at all'. Ultimately he came to a reconciliation with Fox. He married in 1765 Lady Sophia Carteret, the only daughter of Earl Granville; after her death he married in 1779 Lady Louisa Fitzpatrick, the daughter of the first Earl of Upper Ossory. Shelburne died in 1805.

The Duke of Portland
1738 – 1809

Williiam Henry Cavendish Bentinck, third Duke of Portland, was born in 1738, the son of the second Duke. He was educated at Eton and Christ Church, Oxford, and sat in the Commons for Weobly in 1761. In 1762 he succeeded his father. The Portland dynasty was one of the by-products of the Revolution of 1688: almost by birth, Portland was one of the natural leaders of the Whig party. Marriage in 1766 to the daughter of the fourth Duke of Devonshire knitted his links with the other Whig grandees closer still. Rockingham made him Lord Chamberlain in 1765 during his first ministry, and Lord Lieutenant of Ireland in 1782 during his second, and on the death of the Marquess in July 1782 Portland was his natural successor at the head of the Rockingham Whigs.

Charles James Fox, the Rockinghamites' foremost member of the Commons, was the party's real star, as well as its burden. The brilliant and personable Fox, companion in debauchery to the young Prince of Wales, was regarded by the King with intense displeasure: he equally deplored the Rockinghams' willingness to cede independence to America, and their lofty manner towards himself. The circumstances of early 1783, however, left him with little alternative. Fox and Lord North had collaborated (for entirely contrary reasons) in February to secure the rejection of Shelburne's peace treaty. Shelburne resigned, and the King had no option but to accept the coalition into office, decently headed by Portland, as nominal Prime Minister. Fox and North were joint Secretaries of State. The ministry lasted not much longer than its predecessor. Its attempt to settle the debts of the Prince of Wales drove the King to fury; and Fox's proposal to take the affairs of the East India company under parliamentary control presented him with the opportunity to destroy it. Part of the Bill's intention was to entrench the government in power by expanding the sources of patronage. It provoked a storm of controversy; and amid a furious debate about the constitutional proprieties, George III intrigued with the young William Pitt to secure the Bill's rejection in the Lords, and in December he almost casually dismissed the ministry.

Portland remained the figurehead of the party, although the work of opposing Pitt's government fell largely to Fox and Burke. As with others, however – most notably Burke – the French Revolution and its sequel prompted a gradual change in Portland's political attitudes and alliances. Pitt assiduously cultivated Portland and his personal following, and Portland, despite a strong personal attachment to his party, had by January 1794 finally succumbed. The split in the Whigs was opened wider as Fox redoubled the call for parliamentary reform and for peace with France. Portland became Home Secretary, as such responsible for dealing with the Irish insurrection of 1798 and the subsequent Act of Union. An opponent of Pitt's plans for Catholic emancipation, Portland remained in office after Pitt left it over the issue in 1801, and stayed throughout the Addington and second Pitt administrations. On Pitt's death he retired.

The acrimonious collapse in March 1807 of Grenville's 'Ministry of all the Talents' over the King's rejection of their plans for Catholic relief brought Portland back into government. In 1783 Portland's ministry had itself foundered on the hostility of George III; in 1807 Portland took office deliberately in order to defend him from a degrading surrender to his government. Portland's cabinet possessed plenty of talent, with many of Pitt's proteges returning to office: Spencer Perceval as Chancellor of the Exchequer, Canning at the Foreign Office, Castlereagh at the War Office, and Lord Hawkesbury (later the Earl of Liverpool) at the Home Office carried the weight of the government. But riven by internecine squabbles, it collaborated uneasily, and Portland, quite seriously ill and almost ignored by the rest of them, had little hope of holding it together. The ministry had little voting strength in the Commons and was reliant on independent support: it underwent a gruelling session of Parliament, with debates lasting well into the morning. With Portland obviously dying, the disputes over policy and personality between Canning and Castlereagh reached their climax in the struggle for the succession, and culminated in the duel on Putney Heath in September 1809. The ministry fell apart in confusion; Portland resigned, as his health finally gave way. He died on 29 October.

Portland was a shy man, petrified of speaking in public. His premierships were little more than nominal: his qualification for leadership lay in his eminence, not in his ability, and he was kept in the job by a sense of *noblesse oblige* rather than by enjoyment or ambition. In 1766 he had written to Newcastle 'I consider myself as a servant of the Party and shall always think it my duty to act in the manner that is most conducive to its support'; by 1807 he had abandoned his party and took office out of a personal sense of obligation towards the King. Over the intervening forty years, Portland's sense of duty and loyalty had detached themselves from his party and been transferred to the King.

William Pitt (the Younger)
1759 – 1806

William Pitt was born in May 1759, the *annus mirabilis* both of the Seven Years' War and of his father, William Pitt, later Earl of Chatham. Pitt's fond father had early marked out the sickly but precocious child for a brilliant political career, though he left him little else in the way of an inheritance. He was educated at Pembroke Hall, Cambridge, and shortly after his father's death was called to the bar. In 1781 he was elected to the House of Commons at Appleby, and immediately made an impact. Loosely attached to the remaining band of his father's former followers, now led by Lord Shelburne, Pitt made clear his independence and established a reputation as one of the most persistent parliamentary supporters of the movement for parliamentary reform. In 1783 Pitt accepted Shelburne's invitation to become Chancellor of the Exchequer and the ministry's leader in the Commons, aged only twenty-three. The ministry came to grief over Shelburne's proposals for peace with America: his resignation, in February 1783, was followed by Pitt's.

Pitt turned down the King's request that he form a government, and despite all that the King could do to prevent it, the coalition of Lord North and Charles James Fox, decently presided over by the Duke of Portland, was brought into existence. George III sought to strangle it as soon as possible, and found an efficient assassin in Pitt, and a suitable opportunity in Fox's bill to put into order the affairs of the East India company. Despite waging an enormous rhetorical struggle with Fox in the Commons, Pitt failed to defeat the Bill there, but with the assistance of his cousin, Earl Temple, and clear indications of the King's opposition, it was dispatched in the Lords. In December the King dismissed the coalition and made the twenty-five year old Pitt first Lord of the Treasury and Chancellor of the Exchequer.

Pitt's position was tenuous: the King's underhand rejection of the East India Bill raised a fury of constitutional outrage, and Pitt had few dependable allies to take the cabinet posts and little reliable support in the House of Commons. But over the next few months he rode out defeat after defeat, while beating Fox in the appeal for the sympathy and confidence of the independent members and of the public at large. Not until March did he finally dissolve Parliament. The election which followed gave him an astonishing victory, sweeping out of the Commons many of Fox's supporters.

Pitt was to be in office continuously for the next sixteen years. His immediate priority was to reduce the enormous burden of the debt resulting from the American war: he introduced a series of new taxes (including the notorious window tax), and in 1786 reformed the sinking fund. More gradually, Pitt sought to overcome the diplomatic isolation in which Britain had found herself at the end of the War of Independence and to reorganise a colonial system shattered by the loss of America. One step towards that was a settlement of the affairs of the East India Company which, avoiding the controversial system of political control embedded in Fox's 1784 bill, increased the Crown's political authority in India. The efforts of Fox and Edmund Burke to use the impeachment of Warren Hastings as a stick with which to beat Pitt's Indian policy failed when, completely unexpectedly, the Prime Minister associated himself with the prosecution. In the early 1780s Pitt had twice unsuccessfully put forward proposals for parliamentary reform. His third attempt, in April 1785, was to be his last, and Pitt was well aware in advance that it stood little chance of acceptance. After his defeat, he never returned to the issue. Slavery was a different matter, and Pitt backed the campaign against it of his friend, William Wilberforce. By the end of the 1780s, Pitt's dominance in the Commons was assured. The only threat to his position came from the recurrence in 1788 of George III's mental illness. Should he become incapable of government, his son, the Prince of Wales, would become Regent; but the Prince, a friend of Fox's, and closely linked to the Whigs, would, given the chance, expel Pitt and his cronies. Pitt tried to place restrictions on the Regent's powers; but the King's recovery, just as he was plunging into an enormous row with the Prince, dispelled his fears, and disappointed Fox's hopes.

From 1791, British politics were overshadowed by the reverberations of the Revolution in France. Towards the end of 1792, Britain was dragged into continental war against the revolutionary government, formally as a consequence of obligations to the Netherlands under Pitt's Triple Alliance of 1788, but as much because of concern at the efforts of the republicans to export their revolution. With the war came a reaction against the movements which had sprung up in support and celebration of the Revolution. Suspecting the French of fomenting insurrection in Britain, the government clamped down heavily on political dissent with a series of (generally unsuccessful) trials of the leaders of the more radical reform organisations. In the course of 1793 and early 1794 Pitt teased away at the divisions over the war and reform that were now emerging among the Foxite Whigs, welcoming the Duke of Portland and a number of others into his government after a long courtship. The war on the continent went badly: one by one, the members of the European coalition against France of 1793 succumbed to her power. The financial strain on the government was enormous. In 1797 the Bank of England was forced to abandon cash payments, and in 1798 Pitt introduced an income tax. Nelson's destruction of the French fleet at the battle of the Nile in August 1798, however, marked a small turning point. A new alliance against France was built – although that, too, was to be crushed by Bonaparte, leaving Britain by 1801 once more standing alone.

Throughout the 1790s, Pitt's ministry seemed impregnable; the Whigs were in disarray, and the 1796 General Election confirmed his ascendancy; the King's confidence seemed unbounded. It was not the diplomatic and military failures of the war which pushed Pitt out of office, but Ireland. The concession of the franchise to Catholics in 1793 had failed to buy off the strengthening Irish reform movement. In 1798 a conspiracy for a rebellion with assistance from France was uncovered; Pitt concluded that British control over Ireland could be maintained only by a formal union of the two countries and of their two Parliaments; an essential corollary was full emancipation for the Catholic Irish. Catholic emancipation within a British Parliament should, he reasoned, present no threat to the Protestant ascendancy, for the Catholics at Westminster would be too diluted to make much difference. The King thought differently, and insisted that he drop emancipation from the Union scheme. Pitt obeyed; but after the first Union Parliament met in January 1801 Pitt and his cabinet tried again to bring forward measures for Catholic relief. In doing so, he broke the firm partnership with the King which had provided the essential foundation for his ministry since 1784. The King announced indignantly that 'I shall reckon any man my personal enemy who proposes any such measure. The most Jacobinical thing I ever heard of.' Pitt resigned in February.

The King entrusted the government to one of Pitt's friends, the former Speaker Addington. Pitt lent the new ministry his support through the negotiations for the Treaty of Amiens of 1802. But the cordiality was short-lived. Ultimately Pitt joined his old colleagues (especially Lord Grenville and Henry Dundas) in assailing the inadequacies of Addington's administration. In May 1804 it collapsed. Pitt returned to government, but at the head of a feeble ministry. The King's refusal to employ Fox put paid to the hope that a grand coalition might be constructed, and prevented the return of his former Foreign Secretary, Grenville. Pitt was even grateful that Addington would accept office and a peerage at the end of 1804; but the impeachment of Henry Dundas for peculation resulted not merely in his departure from government, but also the resignation of Addington, whose part in Dundas's downfall Pitt much resented. While political factions manoeuvred at Westminster, Bonaparte prepared for the invasion of England, and Spain prepared to enter the war. In the course of 1805 a new coalition was constructed of Britain, Russia, Sweden and Austria, and the battle of Trafalgar put Bonaparte's invasion plans out of the question; but the third coalition began to disentangle with the defeat of Austria and Russia at Austerlitz.

Pitt became seriously ill towards the end of 1805; in January 1806, at one of the worst points of the war, he died, still only forty-six years old. His brilliance was obvious to his contemporaries: his intellect, his self-control, his rhetorical powers were almost legendary; the fact that he appeared to lack any personal warmth only served to confirm his reputation for rigid determination and ruthless efficiency. In fact he was far more human: he couldn't do sums, was hopelessly disorganised and drank too much (he had great drinking bouts with Dundas and with Addington when Speaker). But Pitt was clearly a prodigy. His principal achievements – financial reform, the India Act – lay in peacetime, and as a wartime Minister his command of strategy was indifferent: but, more important, he came to embody the embattled national resolution against the despotism of Bonaparte: 'England has saved herself by her exertions and will, I trust, save Europe by her example'.

Henry Addington
1757 – 1844

Henry Addington was born in 1757, the son of Dr Anthony Addington. He was educated at Winchester School, Lincoln's Inn, and Brasenose College, Oxford. His father, a physician specialising in mental illness, had treated the Earl of Chatham's mysterious complaint, and had become his friend and confidant; Addington himself grew close to Chatham's son, William Pitt. After Pitt became Prime Minister, he encouraged him to enter the House of Commons: he was elected in 1784 for Devizes, and in 1789 Pitt's patronage secured him the Speakership. Patient and courteous, Addington made a good Speaker; but acceptance of the Speakership did not dim his friendship with Pitt, nor preclude him moving into government office. Pitt had seen him for some time as an alternative leader to himself, and when he resigned in February 1801 over the King's refusal to allow Catholic emancipation, George III entrusted Addington, on Pitt's recommendation, with the formation of a 'Protestant' administration. Although Pitt gave him his blessing, most of the leading members of the former ministry were too committed either to Catholic emancipation or to Pitt himself to join him. Addington had to fill up the posts with elder statesmen and his personal cronies.

'Thank God for a government without one of those damned men of genius in it', one member of Parliament was reputed to have said; but the attractions of what seemed (after Pitt) like mediocrity soon wore off. George III's congratulations ('Addington, you have saved the country') were certainly premature. Negotiations for a truce with France had begun under Pitt. Addington was responsible for their conclusion in the Peace of Amiens early in 1802. The large concessions were heavily criticised, particularly by Lord Grenville, Pitt's former Foreign Secretary. The peace was in any case no more than a breathing-space. By May 1803 war had again broken out, and its resumption meant the beginning of the end for Addington's government. The Whigs under Fox, who had supported Addington's peace policy, now denounced his seeming ineptitude in the conduct of the war. Pitt's friends regarded him with contempt. The scorn was scarcely justified, for Addington's achievement in raising finance for the war far exceeded Pitt's; and his military strategy was not obviously any worse. But his performance in the House of Commons was deplorable. Pitt's own decision to join in the condemnation of his former friend finally killed off the government.

Pitt returned to office, though with little solid support in the Commons. Addington still had a substantial party of followers, whose support Pitt was anxious to secure. Addington remained bitter about the way he had been hounded out of office, but the two patched up a reconciliation towards the end of the year, when Addington accepted the Lord Presidency of the Council and (without much enthusiasm, but Pitt wanted him out of the Commons) a peerage as Viscount Sidmouth. It was a shaky alliance. When irregularities were discovered in the naval administration of Pitt's friend, Henry Dundas, Lord Melville, the two again fell out over his prosecution. Sidmouth resigned in July 1805.

After Pitt's death, Sidmouth became Lord Privy Seal, and later Lord President of the Council, in Grenville's 'Ministry of All the Talents', despite his opposition to Grenville's support for Catholic emancipation, and despite Grenville's contempt for him. Addington had been brought into the ministry in order to smooth its relationship with the King; but it was Sidmouth who destroyed it, pointing out to George III the implications of the government's proposals on admitting Catholics to the higher reaches of the army. After his resignation and the collapse of Grenville's ministry, Sidmouth was out of office for five years. But he came back to Perceval's cabinet in 1812, and later that year Pitt's former followers were finally reunited by Lord Liverpool. Sidmouth became Home Secretary, responsible for the government's moves against the Luddite movement and the post-war industrial unrest. Sidmouth gained a reputation for reactionary conservatism: after the Peterloo massacre of 1819 he introduced some of the notorious 'Six Acts' intended to suppress the discontent. He remained at the Home Office for almost ten years until in 1821 he gave it up to make way for Sir Robert Peel. After his retirement from the cabinet in 1827 he took little further part in politics, although he spoke against catholic emancipation in 1829 and voted against the Reform Bill in 1832.

Adddington was remembered as an inept and hapless failure as Prime Minister, and as a reactionary buffoon as Home Secretary. Some of the abuse is attributable to snobbery against the son of a physician (one comment on his elevation to the Lords was 'the son of Lord Chatham's family physician will submit to take a peerage. I give him this description not as considering it to be of any reproach to him, but as a further proof of what the peerage has become of late years'). Some of it reflected his windbaggery at the despatch box. Addington had been the victim of Pitt's ambition, used by him mercilessly for his own purposes, and eventually betrayed. Addington had married in 1791 Ursula Hammond; after her death, he married in 1823 Mary, the daughter of Lord Stowell. He died in 1844.

Lord Grenville
1759 – 1834

William Wyndham Grenville was born in 1759, the youngest son of George Grenville (the Prime Minister in 1763-5) and Elizabeth, the daughter of Sir William Wyndham, and granddaughter of the Duke of Somerset. He was educated at Eton, Christ Church, Oxford, and Lincoln's Inn. Elected to Parliament in 1782 for Buckingham, he was immediately appointed Chief Secretary for Ireland, where his brother, Earl Temple, was Lord Lieutenant. Temple had played a large role in the removal of the Fox-North coalition in 1783 and the rise to power of the Grenvilles' cousin, William Pitt, and Grenville reaped some of the reward. Pitt saw to his rapid promotion: he became Paymaster-General, and in January 1789, aged only thirty, Speaker of the House of Commons. A few months later Pitt moved him on, to become Home Secretary; shortly after that he was raised to the peerage, as Baron Grenville, to be the government's leader in the House of Lords. Pitt, Grenville and Henry Dundas became a governing triumvirate. Grenville's family connections with Pitt were strengthened when in 1792 he married Pitt's cousin, the daughter of Lord Camelford.

In June 1791 Grenville went to the Foreign Office, where he faced the crisis in European politics caused by the convulsions in France. To Grenville fell a large part of the burden of contriving a diplomatic strategy to fight the war against the French republic which broke out in 1793. Closely identified with Pitt's Irish policy, he resigned with the Prime Minister in February 1801 on the King's rejection of Catholic emancipation. But once out of office, Pitt's followers grew apart. Grenville bitterly attacked the concessions to the French in Addington's Peace of Amiens in 1802 ('an act of weakness and humiliation'), and condemned what he saw as Addington's ineptitude. Pitt's slowness to declare his opposition to the government left Grenville, searching about for some means of prising it out of office, to gravitate towards a rather uncomfortable alliance with the opposition Foxite Whigs, whose distaste for the war did not preclude attacking the government over the strategy to be adopted in waging it.

Pitt's decision to bring his weight down on the side of this combination brought Addington's resignation in 1804. Grenville, like Pitt, had hoped for a grand coalition to replace him: Grenville, indeed, had made something of a point of demanding a government gathered from all factions and containing all men of ability, rather than one in which a single minister dominated. But the King put paid to any 'ministry of all the talents' by his insistence that Fox be excluded; and Pitt's undertaking to the King that he would not press for Catholic emancipation pushed Grenville further from alliance with his former chief.

On Pitt's death, in January 1806, Grenville appeared to be the only leader who could attract the loyalty of the present ministers; George III reluctantly accepted his determination to make his government as widely based as possible, even if it meant including the awful Fox, as Foreign Secretary. In the end, though, Grenville failed to attract 'all the talents': many of Pitt's most able followers held themselves aloof from a government in which Fox was so prominent. While Grenville left Fox to manage foreign affairs, and to make new approaches to Bonaparte for peace, he himself took steps to set Britain on a firmer footing at home on the assumption that the war would continue. Neither man was particularly successful: the negotiations with France soon foundered, and the government's military strategy seemed piecemeal and ineffective against the confident advance of Bonaparte in Europe. Grenville's army reforms were over-hastily drafted, and aroused bitter resistance. The ministry's only real achievement was the full abolition of the British Slave Trade.

The government fell, as had Pitt's in 1801, on the issue of Catholic relief. In its first year, Grenville had tried to balance the competing interests in Ireland of Catholics and Protestants. But a revival of Irish Catholic agitation in early 1807 — as well as the need to strengthen the army with Irish Catholic levies — upset Grenville's Irish 'system' and convinced him that a series of concessions were essential. In his attempt to bring the King around to the same view, Grenville provoked a confrontation with him. In the middle of March he and his government were dismissed.

For the next ten years, Grenville was the acknowledged leader of the main body of the Whig opposition, dominating the alliance between his own and the Foxite groups by reason of his political and intellectual influence, despite his lack of enthusiasm for the role. The opportunity which the opposition saw to come to power in 1811, when George III's illness necessitated the regency of his son, was largely lost because of Grenville's insensitivity and inflexibility, as well as the Prince of Wales's objections to his pro-catholicism. In the years after Waterloo, Grenville moved away from the Whigs, and closer to the Liverpool government, particularly impelled by his concern for law and order during the post-war unrest. He abandoned his leadership of the opposition in 1817, and by 1821 was willing to lend his support to Lord Liverpool. In 1823 he suffered a stroke, and retired from public life.

Grenville was, as he himself admitted, 'not competent for the management of men', and indeed, it was a lack of skill in managing the King, as much as anything else, which wrecked his ministry. He claimed to dislike the premiership, and was relieved to abandon it, while he found formal opposition distasteful. Part of the reason he stayed in politics at all was money: lacking the solid financial base of a large estate, he needed office to keep him solvent. He died in 1834.

Spencer Perceval
1762 – 1812

Spencer Perceval was born in 1762, the son of the Earl of Egmont and his second wife, Catherine Compton. He was educated at Harrow and Trinity College, Cambridge, and began a practice at the bar. Two pamphlets, one on the constitutional arguments surrounding the impeachment of Warren Hastings, and the other on the practicalities of prosecuting those charged with sedition and other offences related to the reform agitation of the early 1790s, brought him prominence and the prosecution brief at the trial of Thomas Paine and Horne Tooke. In 1796 he was made a King's Counsel, and in the same year was elected to the House of Commons for Northampton.

Perceval entered the House dedicated to his patron, Pitt and to the war with revolutionary France. He was, however, also a strong evangelical Churchman, and profoundly opposed to Pitt's proposal for Catholic emancipation. On Pitt's resignation over the issue in 1801, Perceval accepted the post of solicitor general in Addington's government. In 1802 he was promoted to be the government's senior counsel, and he retained the office on Pitt's return to power in 1804. Perceval's evangelical views drew him to support the campaigns of William Wilberforce for the abolition of the slave trade and (rather less vigorously) for the amelioration of the position of children at work.

After Pitt's death, Perceval, along with a number of his other former proteges, resigned from government, rather than take office with Charles James Fox. Perceval was again prominent in the opposition to Grenville's plans to allow Catholics to hold senior commissions in the army, the rock on which his ministry foundered. In the administration which followed, he accepted the Chancellorship, and became the ministry's leader in the Commons. The feuds between Canning and Castlereagh, drawing Perceval in, wrecked the government's cohesion and brought it to an end in 1809. Portland's resignation left no very obvious successor. The King fixed on Perceval; his rivals, Canning and Castlereagh, resigned, and it was with extreme difficulty that Perceval succeeded in constructing a government at all.

With little to recommend it but the widely acknowledged integrity of its chief, Perceval's ministry limped desperately through its first year. Lord Wellesley, Wellington's brother, ran the Foreign Office with incompetence and squabbled with his colleagues over the war with Spain; the government came once more under enormous pressure for parliamentary reform; and Perceval, never popular with the Prince of Wales after his defence of the Prince's wife, Princess Caroline, in 1805-7 against charges of adultery, incurred his further displeasure over the arrangements for the regency on the King's decline into madness at the end of 1810. In any case, the Prince's old friendship with many of the leading Whigs seemed likely to expel the government as soon as he took full charge. But during the course of 1811, the Prince developed at least a working relationship with Perceval, and when he assumed full powers in early 1812, Perceval was retained, and Wellesley, who had intrigued against him, was forced to resign. The ministry was strengthened with the addition of Lord Sidmouth and Castlereagh.

Perceval's position was now rather more secure. However on 11 May, he was assassinated in the lobby of the House of Commons by John Bellingham, a crazed merchant with a personal grievance against the government. To many of his contemporaries, Perceval was ordinary: he had, said Sydney Smith, 'the head of a country parson and the tongue of an Old Bailey lawyer'; George III called him 'the most straightforward man he had ever known'. Perceval may have been unspectacular; but in a determined and routine sort of way, he was highly efficient, and also (as contemporaries frequently noted) clearly a man of integrity. He died on the verge of final victory in the long war against France, as the vast sums which his ministry had poured into backing Wellington in Spain and Portugal were beginning to bear fruit. He had married in 1790 Jane, the daughter of Sir Thomas Wilson.

The Earl of Liverpool
1770 – 1828

Robert Banks Jenkinson, second Earl of Liverpool, was born in 1770, the son of the first Earl, who had been widely regarded by the opposition in the late 1770s as George III's principal confidant. Jenkinson was educated at Charterhouse and at Christ Church, Oxford. European travel took him to Paris at the fall of the Bastille in 1789, and into the acquaintance of some of the leaders of the French royalist party. In 1795 he married Louisa, the daughter of the Earl (and Bishop) of Bristol. He was elected to the House of Commons for Rye in 1790. In 1793 he was taken into office, at the India Board, in the administration in which his father was President of the Board of Trade. Except for a brief period in 1806, he remained in government until 1827. Known as Lord Hawkesbury after his father took a peerage, he became Foreign Secretary in Addington's ministry of 1801, a position which gave him some of the responsibility, and the odium, for negotiating the Peace of Amiens. In 1803 Addington raised him to the peerage in his own right. On Pitt's return to power in 1804, he took the Home Secretaryship.

With Pitt's death, Hawkesbury left office, leading the opposition to Grenville in the Lords. He returned to government in March 1807, again as Home Secretary, as part of the reunion of 'Pitt's friends' under the Duke of Portland. Hawkesbury, Earl of Liverpool after his father's death in 1808, adhered to Perceval and stayed in office after Portland's government had been smashed by the rivalry of Castlereagh and Canning. He moved to be Secretary of State for War and the Colonies, solidly backing Wellington's campaigns in Spain and Portugal by refusing to divert scarce resources elsewhere. After Perceval's assassination, he was acting Prime Minister; the subsequent failure of either Canning, the principal member of Pitt's old faction still outside government, or the Whigs under Grenville and Grey to form an administration, left him fully in power.

Catholic emancipation had been one of the main blocks to the reuniting of Pitt's old allies. Liverpool declared it to be a matter not of cabinet policy, but of individual conscience; on that understanding, he was able to attract to his government both Lord Sidmouth and Castlereagh, at either ends of the argument, and to discourage Canning from active opposition. But despite the reunion of 'Pitt's friends', the government still lacked firm and reliable support in the Commons, and depended on the informal support of uncommitted members.

Confirmed in power at the General Election of 1812, Liverpool's government presided over the defeat of Napoleon. Repulsed from Russia and chased out of Spain, the Emperor was forced to abdicate in April 1814; his brief reappearance and defeat at Waterloo in 1815 disposed of him for ever, leaving British power dominant in Europe. Peace meant the settling of the nation's accounts: the demand for an instant reduction in the tax burden and the defeat of the government's proposal for a renewal of the income tax in 1816 placed it in desperate financial straits until the early 1820s. Liverpool responded firmly to the wave of discontent and the growth of radicalism which attended the savage post-war recession. A series of measures against sedition were hurried through

Parliament in 1817, including the suspension of Habeas Corpus; in 1819, in the aftermath of the violent suppression of a public meeting in St Peter's Fields, Manchester (the 'Peterloo Massacre'), a further programme of repressive measures (the 'Six Acts') was enacted. Agricultural depression produced distress in the countryside, and pressure for corn imports to be restricted in order to hold up the price of English grain. Liverpool, though deeply read in the political economists and strongly attached to the principle of free trade, accepted in 1815 the prohibition of corn imports under a fixed price – the first of the Corn Laws – as, he hoped, an interim measure to encourage the revival of English agriculture. Some efforts were made to alleviate the suffering of the poor – among them the 1817 Poor Employment Act, which offered a scheme to encourage work-creating projects – but their extent was limited both by a belief that government intervention could achieve little and by a shortage of money with which to intervene.

One matter gave Liverpool almost as much trouble as the entire peace settlement – the divorce of George IV. On his accession in 1820, the position of the King's estranged wife, Caroline ('the most impudent devil that ever lived', according to the Duke of Wellington), became particularly awkward. Liverpool tried, but failed, to achieve a compromise short of divorce; that failing, the government placed evidence before the House of Lords concerning her conduct, and brought in a bill to deprive her of her title and dignities as Queen, and to divorce her from the King. A wave of public sympathy for Caroline (and also of disgust for the King, whose philandering had been no better than hers) forced Liverpool to withdraw the Bill, to George IV's anger. His relationship with Liverpool never quite mended. The affair also resulted in the resignation of Canning – though he was to return in 1822 as Foreign Secretary.

The return of Canning (one of Liverpool's oldest friends), placed an enormous strain on the ministry. Now Leader of the House of Commons, Canning's weight shifted the balance of the cabinet towards favouring Catholic relief just as a renewal of Catholic agitation in Ireland under Daniel O'Connell and the Catholic Association brought the issue back into the limelight. The cabinet's agreement to differ on Catholic emancipation was almost destroyed, as Canning supported the package of three bills to remove Catholic disabilities brought forward in 1825, and the cabinet began to split into 'Catholic' and 'Protestant' wings (the latter headed by Peel). Liverpool barely succeeded in keeping it together. Canning's rhetorical adoption of 'liberal' objectives in foreign policy equally strained the loyalty of other members of the cabinet. Towards the end of his ministry, another of the government's long-running problems revived: a shortage of corn following the bad harvest of 1825 stimulated demands for the abolition of the Corn Laws. In collaboration with Canning, Peel and Huskisson (the free-trader who was President of the Board of Trade), Liverpool drew up a scheme designed to balance protection of the landed interest when prices were low with ensuring the availability of corn during periods of dearth – the so-called 'sliding scale' for import duties. But Liverpool's health was already failing, and before the Bill could be introduced, in February 1827, he suffered a stroke and tendered his resignation.

Liverpool had held the premiership for fifteen years, longer than anyone but Walpole and Pitt. He was respected for his integrity, calmness and good temper, although he became fidgety under stress, and was determinedly unsociable. On his arrival in office, he had been faced with a country struggling with the social and economic consequences of war; by 1825 it was basking in 'unprecedented, unparalleled prosperity' – although the dawn proved false when recession returned that year. In his recognition of the value of the commercial interest and the case for free-trade, Liverpool laid the foundations for the doctrines on which Peel was to attempt to refashion the Conservative party twenty years after his death. Liverpool's first wife had died in 1821. He married again, in 1822, her friend and companion, Mary Chester. Liverpool died only a few months after his resignation.

George Canning
1770 – 1827

George Canning was born in 1770, the son of George Canning and Mary Anne Costello. His father, a lawyer and apostle of John Wilkes, had been disinherited by his own stern and unforgiving father, and died in 1771 in poverty; his mother, to survive, went on the stage. Canning was brought up by his uncle, Stratford Canning, a prosperous London merchant. He was educated at Eton, at Christ Church, Oxford, and at Lincoln's Inn. His uncle had strong connections with the Foxite Whigs, and the young George Canning, too, became friends with Fox, Lord and Lady Holland, and other Whig luminaries; but the French Revolution, Whig dabbling in parliamentary reform, and the attractions of working with William Pitt turned him Tory. In 1793 he entered Parliament; he attached himself to Pitt and became one of his young proteges. In 1796 Pitt secured for him the place of Under-Secretary of State for foreign affairs.

While holding it, Canning helped to found the anti-revolutionary newspaper, the Anti-Jacobin, and was one of its principal contributors. He and Pitt became extremely close; Pitt even helped him to his marriage, to Joan Scott, the heiress of Major-General John Scott, in 1800. When Pitt left the government in 1801, Canning insisted on resigning too, having strongly supported Pitt's project of Catholic emancipation (his mother came from an Irish Catholic background). With Pitt he returned to office in 1804, and was made Treasurer of the Navy.

Pitt's death left him miserable, confessing to 'a feeling of loneliness and dismay which I have never felt half so strongly before'. He resigned, and set about attacking Grenville's 'Talents' ministry. In Portland's reunion of 'Pitts's friends' in the government of 1809, Canning was appointed Foreign Secretary. His relationship with Castlereagh, who at the War Office shared with Canning most of the administrative burden of the war with France, was one of the most unhappy features of an unhappy ministry. Their conflicts of personality and policy came to a head with a duel on Putney Heath in September 1809; Canning was slightly wounded, and the ministry was mortally so. Portland, whose mismanagement of their rivalry had contributed to the ugliness of its denouement, resigned because of ill-health in October. Canning lost out to Perceval in the struggle for the succession; he failed again on Perceval's assassination. Still preserving his rather petulant rivalry with Castlereagh, he effectively excluded himself from the new government of the Earl of Liverpool. For a time he left politics and the country altogether. During 1813 his little faction was disbanded, and over the next year its members were absorbed into the government.

By 1816, the sting of the quarrels with Castlereagh had faded sufficiently to enable him to accept a place in the cabinet and the Presidency of the Board of Control. But another stroke of ill-fortune – the 'trial' of Queen Caroline – soon appeared to have wrecked his political career for a second time. Canning had been her friend (there were rumours that he had been her lover), and his opposition to the proceedings against her led him to resign in December 1820, giving the King profound offence. Canning was on the verge of departing to the Governor-Generalship of India and the political wilderness when Castlereagh's suicide, in August 1822, transformed the situation. Liverpool managed to browbeat the King into accepting Canning as the replacement Foreign Secretary and Leader of the House of Commons.

Canning as Foreign Secretary was brilliant, flamboyant and an enormous burden to his colleagues. Courting popular liberalism, he gained a reputation as the champion of nationalist and democratic resistance to the continental autocracies. In reality, his support for the democrats was more limited, and his views less liberal than they seemed. He condemned the French intervention against the Spanish revolution of 1823, but did nothing to prevent it; his recognition of the revolted Spanish colonies of Latin America was prompted by calculations of commercial advantage; and the naval intervention to protect Portuguese independence against Spanish interference was intended to prevent the French intervening first. In responding to the aftermath of the Greek revolt of 1821 against Turkish domination, Canning balanced popular philhellenism with the strategic realities: there was no question of offering British assistance to the Greeks (whom he regarded as 'a most rascally sort'). Canning sought to mediate, while carefully maintaining the delicate balance of power in the Eastern Mediterranean against the possibility of Russian intervention. By the Treaty of London of 1827 he allied with Russia and France to end the war – if necessary using force. In the event, the Treaty was something of an own goal. When the Turks refused to accept a ceasefire, the allies were bound to intervene: the result was the destruction of the Turkish fleet, and a self-inflicted blow to British power in the Mediterranean.

Canning's appointment had shattered the peace of the Liverpool cabinet. His intrigues, his meddling, his corrosive wit, were all irritating enough to his colleagues; but more seriously, the strength of his pro-Catholic sympathies almost wrecked the agreement to differ on the question of Catholic emancipation on which the Liverpool government had been founded. Canning's support for Sir Francis Burdett's bills on Catholic relief in 1825 stimulated a cabinet crisis barely soothed over by Liverpool's diplomacy; so when, in early 1827, Liverpool was forced to resign because of ill-health, and the new King, William IV, asked Canning to form a ministry, half the cabinet resigned, with Wellington and Peel leading the exodus of its 'Protestant' wing.

Canning managed instead to construct a government by attracting the support of the moderate Whigs under the leadership of the Marquess of Lansdowne. However four months later, Canning was dead, of a chill, so it was said, caught at the funeral of the Duke of York. There had been time to do nothing, save to be defeated on the Corn Law Bill which Liverpool had been preparing before his own death.

Canning never quite overcame his origins – Wellington called him a 'charlatan parvenu' – but what he lacked in social standing, he made up for in talent and hard work. His reputation was made as Foreign Secretary, not in his brief tenure of the premiership. If his liberalism was more rhetorical than actual, he nevertheless brought a dramatic new populist style to his office, an alertness to the uses to which public opinion might be put, which was radically different to that of his predecessor, Castlereagh. For all his rhetorical populism and fondness for the grand gesture, Canning was thoroughly level-headed in his attitude to policy issues. 'The duty of a British statesman', he claimed, was 'to hold a middle course between extremes, avoiding alike extravagancies of despotism, or the licentiousness of unbridled freedom'.

Viscount Goderich
1782 – 1859

Frederick John Robinson, Viscount Goderich, was born in 1782, the younger son of the second Lord Grantham, Foreign Secretary under Lord Shelburne. He was educated at Harrow and St John's College, Cambridge. In 1803 he was made secretary to his cousin, the Earl of Hardwicke, then Lord Lieutenant of Ireland. In 1806 he was elected to the House of Commons for an Irish seat, although after the General Election of May 1807 he represented Ripon. In Portland's government he found office, as Under-Secretary for the Colonies, and a mentor, Viscount Castlereagh, the Secretary at War. At about the same time, Robinson began to meet regularly with other young Tories, including Peel, at the Alfred Club, and they came to form a close political group. Robinson resigned with Castlereagh in 1809. He was brought back into the Perceval government in 1810 by his relation, Charles Yorke, and continued in office, as

Vice-President of the Board of Trade, in Liverpool's. For a few months in 1813–14 he accompanied Castlereagh to France to begin the diplomatic negotiations following the defeat of Bonaparte. In 1814 he married Sarah, the daughter and heiress of the Earl of Buckinghamshire.

Robinson's personal views, and his position, made him one of the principal advocates of the Liverpool government's liberal commercial policy, and it was with some reluctance that he took responsibility in the Commons for the Corn Law Bill of 1815. By 1818 he had taken full control of the Board of Trade. In the government reshuffle made necessary by Castlereagh's suicide in 1822, he became Chancellor of the Exchequer. An economic recovery after the post-war recession enabled him to make deep tax cuts in his budget of 1823, which won him the nickname 'Prosperity' Robinson and a rising reputation, but the end of the boom in 1825 and a financial crisis saw his star sinking again. The death of his daughter and the onset of his wife's insanity left him by 1826 anxious to leave politics altogether.

Liverpool's cabinet had become hopelessly divided after 1825 over Canning's support for Catholic emancipation; when in April 1827 the Prime Minister resigned out of ill health, and was replaced by Canning, the 'Protestant' wing of the government trooped out, en bloc. One of the more cautious supporters of Catholic relief, Robinson accepted Canning's offer of a peerage as Viscount Goderich, appointment as Secretary of State for War and the Colonies and the leadership of the House of Lords. When Canning died, only a few months later, the King turned to Goderich. He inherited Canning's alliance with the moderate Whigs. But his personality was neither commanding nor charismatic enough to animate an administration paralysed by suspicions between Tories and Whigs, 'Protestants' and pro-emancipationists, between those who rejoiced at and those who deplored the Anglo-French defeat of Turkey at Navarino in October. The constant vexation of cabinet politics combined with his wife's state of mental confusion to reduce the Prime Minister to what Huskisson, the Colonial Secretary, described as 'a most pitiful state'; but it was Huskisson who lost his nerve first and resigned in the belief that the government would simply collapse as soon as the new session of Parliament began. The tottering ministry was finally pushed over by a direct challenge from its ultra-Tory Chancellor, Herries. In January 1828 Goderich, allegedly in tears, met the King, and left having either resigned, or been dismissed – no-one was quite sure which.

In the cabinet of Whigs and Cannings' followers which Earl Grey assembled in 1830, Goderich took his old position, of Secretary of State for War and the Colonies. His acceptance was accompanied by a rather grudging conversion to parliamentary reform, as a necessary, if not a desirable measure. His office gave him the responsibility for implementing the government's policy of abolishing slavery in the colonies, but he agreed, unhappily, to exchange it for the post of Lord Privy Seal in April 1833, when it seemed necessary to make room in the government for Lord Stanley, despite an awareness that he would be seen as running away from the enormous difficulties of implementing the slavery scheme. Though compensated with a new title, as Earl of Ripon, he found himself an increasingly marginal figure, and a year later he left the government altogether, finally alienated by the comments of Lord Russell on the disposal of the surplus revenues of the Irish Church. His resignation (along with those of three colleagues) precipitated the fall of Grey's government a few weeks later.

Ripon gravitated back towards the Conservatives. He took office for the last time in the second administration of Sir Robert Peel in September 1841, as President of the Board of Trade, and subsequently as President of the Board of Control for the affairs of India. He was closely involved with Peel's overhaul of the customs duties along similar lines to a revision for which he had been responsible in the early 1820s. When it came to the Corn Laws, Ripon was at first against the alteration of the sliding scale for corn import duties which was brought in in 1828, but after Peel outfaced the rest of the cabinet on the issue at the end of 1845, he loyally promoted outright repeal in the Lords. He resigned with Peel in June 1846, and took little further part in politics. Ripon was scarcely built for greatness: a capable administrator, he was unable to take the strain of the highest office. His ministry, though, had been destroyed by Catholic emancipation and there was little that he could have done to prevent its demise. He died in 1859.

The Duke of Wellington
1769 – 1852

Arthur Wellesley, first Duke of Wellington, was born in Ireland in 1769, the fourth son of the first Earl of Mornington and Anne, eldest daughter of the Viscount Dungannon. He was educated at Eton, until after his father's death his mother, unable to afford the school any longer, took him with her to Brussels. Commissioned into the army in 1787, he served as Aide-De-Camp to two successive Lords Lieutenant of Ireland. In 1790 he was elected to the Irish Parliament.

War with France gave Wellesley the opportunity for active service. In 1793 he became Lieutenant-Colonel of his regiment, and the following year saw his first fighting against the French in a grim winter campaign in the low countries. In 1796 his regiment was posted to India, where he was to become the unofficial adviser to his brother, the second Earl of Mornington, the Governor-General.

The success of his campaign against the Mahratta states was the beginning of his military reputation. In 1805 he returned to England, and the following year was elected to Parliament. The Duke of Portland offered him the post of Chief Secretary for Ireland, and he accepted, stipulating that he should still be permitted to go abroad on active service.

In July 1808 he sailed to Portugal, to support the Spanish uprising against the Bonapartes. For more than five years, Wellesley fought the French in Portugal and Spain, while struggling with disorganised and suspicious allies and his own government, which was frequently divided on whether the Peninsular War was its strategic priority or not. Following Salamanca in 1812 and Vitoria the following year, the French were finally driven out of Spain towards the end of 1813. Wellesley followed them into France, taking Bayonne and Toulouse before the news came of Napoleon's abdication in April 1814. Created a Viscount in 1809 and Marquess in 1812, on his return to England Wellesley was made Duke of Wellington, and British Ambassador at Paris. Called back from the Congress of Vienna on Napoleon's escape from Elba, Wellington with the Prussian General Blücher inflicted their most famous defeat on the French at Waterloo in June 1815; Paris fell, and the Bourbons were restored. Wellington remained on the continent as Commander-in-Chief of the army of occupation in France until 1818.

Showered with honours and gifts, Wellington was now a rich man, whose national prestige was second to none. He was, in short, not just a national hero, but a national institution. The prestige wore off a little after he was brought into the Liverpool cabinet in 1818 as Master-General of the Ordnance; opposition politicians suspected his ambition and disliked his reactionary views. He battled against democratic agitation at home, liberal and nationalist movements abroad, and the catholic emancipationists in the cabinet. The return of George Canning to the government in 1822 was particularly galling. He bitterly resisted Canning's recognition of the rebel governments in Spain's American colonies and the Treaty of July 1827 which was to bring Britain into conflict with Turkey over the Greek nationalist revolution. On Canning's appointment as prime minister in April 1827, Wellington resigned from the cabinet and from the command of the army.

Goderich's failure to hold together the rump of Liverpool's administration after Canning's death made the King turn to Wellington as a figure who might be able to recreate a strong government after the divisions and weakness of the past year. During January 1828, in close association with Sir Robert Peel, Wellington formed a cabinet which reunited the surviving members of the Liverpool administration. Followers of Canning, particularly William Huskisson and Viscount Palmerston, were included at the insistence of Peel, disappointing those ultra-Tories who had expected a cabinet united in opposition to all kinds of liberalism. The consequence of its inclusiveness was division: Wellington and the Canningites clashed over the support to be given to Greece under the Treaty of 1827; and an argument between them over the details of Huskisson's Corn Law Bill threatened for a time to bring down the government. The Canningites finally left in May after a quarrel over whether the parliamentary seats of two disenfranchised boroughs should be transferred to the expanding industrial towns of Manchester and Birmingham, or reapportioned locally.

Wellington, with Peel, led the 'Protestant' wing of the Liverpool cabinet in its opposition to Catholic emancipation in 1825; but Wellington's resistance to the proposal was even then tempered by a recognition that the Irish Catholic party could never be finally suppressed. The revival of the Catholic Association in Ireland, and the election to Parliament of Daniel O'Connell (who was disqualified as a Catholic) forced the issue back to the top of the political agenda. Wellington and Peel became convinced that without some concession, severe unrest, even revolution, was certain. The situation was particularly awkward for the government: not only had many of those who had pledged their support for Wellington and Peel done so because they believed that they would resist Catholic emancipation, but it was also something to which William IV, like his predecessors, was deeply opposed. In 1829 it brought in a bill suppressing the Catholic Association, another sweeping away all catholic disabilities, and a third which had the effect of radically reducing the Irish electorate – at once conceding emancipation, and overcoming its political effects. Ultra-Tories were incensed by Wellington's betrayal. Lord Winchilsea accused him of dishonesty, and challenged the Prime Minister to a duel. Both men deliberately missed (although

Wellington's aim was notoriously atrocious anyway).

The resentment of the ultras left Wellington's government almost powerless in the Commons, just as the various reactions to Catholic emancipation combined with an economic depression helped to revive discussion of parliamentary reform. The death of George IV in June 1830 entailed a new Parliament: the elections seemed to indicate a mood for change; and Wellington, perversely, resolved that the best means of contesting reform was to meet it head on. In a sensational speech soon after the opening of the Parliament he declared his determination to resist. The government was defeated in the Commons and on 15 November it resigned.

Wellington fought long and hard against Grey's reform bills in the Lords, but with his failure to form a ministry after Grey's resignation in the 'days of May' in 1832 his resistance was at an end, and he absented himself from the remaining proceedings in the Lords. In the early 1830s, Wellington was ceding the leadership of the Tory party to Peel. In 1834 he refused the premiership for himself, but took office as First Lord of the Treasury until the younger man could return from holiday in Italy. For three weeks he ran the government almost single-handed, and on Peel's return, he became Foreign Secretary. In Peel's second ministry, in 1841, Wellington took a seat in the cabinet without office, with the leadership of the Lords, but by now his influence was much reduced. He was appointed Commander-in-Chief of the army for life in 1842, and pressed – vainly – for rearmament. Despite his doubts about Peel's corn law bill of 1846, he loyally supported it. With the resignation of the government in June 1846, Wellington's ministerial career came to an end.

Wellington had married Catherine Pakenham, the daughter of the second Lord Longford, in 1806. The two were profoundly unsuited ('I married her because they asked me to do it and I did not know myself'), and his wife was a constant source of irritation. He kept up a series of friendships with a number of other women, most notably Harriet Arbuthnot, who died in 1833, and Angela Burdett-Coutts, who proposed marriage in 1847, but most oddly, the evangelical Anna Maria Jenkins, who kept up a long correspondence with him in the hope of bringing him to repentance. In politics, Wellington never forgot he was a soldier. Despising the politician's arts of compromise and indifferent to the opinion of the public, Wellington was guided by his strong belief in the necessity of aristocratic leadership and firm government, but while he held strongly illiberal opinions, he had common sense in plenty and an awareness of what was politically realistic. He died in 1852, outliving almost all of his principal protagonists and antagonists, and was buried in great splendour at St Paul's.

The Earl Grey
1764 – 1845

Charles Grey, second Earl Grey, was born in 1764, the son of General Sir Charles, later Earl, Grey, and his wife Elizabeth, daughter of George Grey of Southwick, Durham. Educated at Eton and at King's College, Cambridge, in 1786 he became Member of Parliament for Northumberland. Attaching himself to Charles James Fox, he was prominent in the impeachment of Warren Hastings, and closely involved in the promotion of parliamentary reform. In 1792, along with other young Foxites, he launched the Society of the Friends of the People, dedicated to moderate reform aimed at reducing the excessive influence of the Crown. Grey introduced unsuccessful motions for parliamentary reform in May 1793 and in 1797; he called for peace with France, attacked Pitt's anti-sedition legislation, and in 1800 fought the Bill of Union with Ireland on the grounds that it would lead to the reinforcement of the Crown's influence in the Commons. Grey's marriage in 1794, to Mary Elizabeth Ponsonby, the daughter of the first

Lord Ponsonby, brought him into contact with the leaders of the liberal Irish party. (The marriage also finally put an end to his scandalous affair with Georgiana, Duchess of Devonshire.)

After 1800, Fox and Grey drifted apart, as Grey distanced himself from Fox's demand for peace, and from the more radical proposals for an extension of the franchise. In 1806 he took office in Grenville's 'Ministry of all the Talents', and on Fox's death in September Grey (now known by the courtesy title of Lord Howick following his father's elevation to an earldom) succeeded to both the Foreign Secretaryship and to the Leadership of the House of Commons. Howick had barely time to make an impression on the office before the government was evicted by the King's rejection of its stance on Catholic emancipation.

On his father's death in November 1807, Howick became the second Earl Grey. He inherited on Fox's death a year earlier the leadership of the Whigs; but divided between radicals such as his brother-in-law Samuel Whitbread and the aristocratic Whig grandees, the party proved ineffective in opposition. In early 1809 the radicals virtually seceded from the party altogether. It was unable to capitalise as it might have done on the regency of the Prince of Wales – an old friend of Fox from the 1790s; and after the end of the War with France, the other wing of the opposition, under Lord Grenville, edged closer to the government of Lord Liverpool. Grey himself was an unenthusiastic and often invisible leader of the opposition, preferring a very happy home life at Howick to politics in London. Even in 1804 he had complained of political life as a 'pursuit which I detest, which interferes with all my private comfort, and which I only sigh for an opportunity of abandoning decidedly and for ever'.

The instability of the successive Tory governments after Liverpool's death, the crisis in the Tory party which followed Catholic emancipation, and the severe economic depression which began to bite in the late 1820s created the conditions for a return of the Whigs to power after a quarter of a century in opposition. The election of the summer of 1830 made necessary by the death of George IV produced a Parliament receptive to reform. Wellington's startling announcement of his steadfast opposition to it brought his government down in November.

Grey was asked to form a cabinet. He added some Tories and Canningites to the Whigs to overcome their lack of ministerial experience. The appointment of the reformer, Henry Brougham, as chancellor, however, clearly indicated the government's intentions. The first Reform Bill was introduced in the Commons by Lord John Russell in March 1831, and received a second reading by a majority of only one. Grey asked for, and got, a dissolution; in the ensuing general election, fought directly on the issue of reform, he secured a clear majority. The second Reform Bill easily passed the Commons in July; but with Wellington leading the opposition in the Lords, it was rejected there in October. Grey patiently brought in a third bill in early 1832. Again it was effectively lost in the Lords. In early May, unable to persuade William IV to use the threat of creating peers to force the Lords to accept the bill, the ministry resigned. In a few days of high drama, the 'days of May', the King found that no alternative ministry could be formed, and he was forced to accept Grey and his colleagues back and to agree to swamp the Lords with new peers if necessary. The threat was enough to overcome the opposition to the Bill, which was passed, to great rejoicing, in June 1832.

The first election held on the new franchise in December 1832 brought home the extent of the change wrought by the Reform Act not only on the electoral system, but also on the Whigs. The radical complexion of the new Parliament pushed the government towards further reforms: the abolition of slavery in the colonies, the Factory Act of 1833, and the beginnings of a reorganisation of municipal government. The uneasy relationship between radicals and conservatives in the Whig party ultimately broke down over Lord John Russell's scheme for parliamentary appropriation of the tithes of the Irish Anglican Church. In May 1834 Lords Ripon and Stanley resigned, taking with them the conservative wing. Further difficulties over the proposal provoked Grey — gratefully — to resign in July.

Grey lived until 1845. Though brief, his premiership saw the passage of a measure which was to transform British political life. Grey had supported reform, in order to preserve the constitution. For him, the 1832 Act was final; for many of his more radical colleagues, it was only a beginning.

The Viscount Melbourne
1779 – 1848

William Lamb, second Viscount Melbourne, the second son of the first Viscount and Elizabeth, the daughter of Sir Ralph Milbanke, was born in 1779. He was educated at Eton, Trinity College, Cambridge, Glasgow University and Lincoln's Inn. The death of his elder brother in 1806 prompted Lamb to abandon the bar and take a seat in the House of Commons, for Leominster. His parents were both close to the circle of the Prince of Wales (it was rumoured that his mother was the Prince's mistress) and Lamb fell early into an attachment to the Foxite Whigs; in many respects he shared the liberal instincts of their radical wing, but, strongly opposed to parliamentary reform, his relationship with the party was equivocal. The complexities of his attitude (as well as the complexities of his wife, the notorious Lady Caroline Lamb, the daughter of the Earl of Bessborough whom he married in 1805) contributed to his absence from Parliament from 1812 to 1816: when he returned, his distaste for the popular unrest which accompanied the post-war depression helped him to slide towards an association with the Canningite wing of the Tories. Canning made him Chief Secretary for Ireland in 1827, and he retained office under Wellington, although (like the other Canningites) his alliance with the Tories was an uneasy one: they resigned, en bloc, in 1828. On his father's death the following year he took his seat in the House of Lords.

Melbourne was gathered back into the bosom of the Whigs when the Canningites were subsumed into Grey's government in November 1830. Melbourne became Home Secretary, a grudging convert to a reform of Parliament which he now conceded could scarcely be avoided, but which he still feared could result in 'a prevalence of the blackguard interest'. On Grey's resignation in July 1834, the King called on Melbourne, as the leader of the more moderate Whigs, to lead a coalition with Wellington and Peel; but the suggestion was an impractical one when the parties were so signally at odds over the reform of the Irish Church, and Melbourne became Premier at the head of a cabinet similar to Grey's. He was no more successful than Grey had been at balancing moderates and the more thoroughgoing reformers among the Whigs; the strength of the latter made William IV nervous, and he dispatched the ministry in November, having refused to allow Melbourne to appoint Lord John Russell leader of the Commons.

With the Tories vastly outnumbered by the opposition they were unlikely to survive long in office, even after their gains in Peel's election of January 1835. Over the winter of 1834-5 Melbourne forged a new alliance between the Whigs, the radicals and Daniel O'Connell's Irish party; in retrospect, it appeared as the moment at which the Victorian Liberal party was formed, giving the Whigs a clear identity as the party of further reform. Peel's government fell in April 1835, and the King reluctantly accepted back Melbourne and the Whigs. Predictably, Melbourne's alliance with the Irish quickly forced his government into the quagmire of Church reform: Russell's repeated efforts to secure parliamentary appropriation of the excess revenues of the Church of Ireland were swamped by the conservative majority in the Lords. Having divided the cabinet and wrecked the government's legislative programme, the issue was finally dropped in 1838. By contrast, the English Municipal Reform Bill, adjusting the franchise for local elections, secured a comparatively easy passage, with the cooperation of Peel.

The death of William IV in June 1837 and the accession of Queen Victoria changed the nature of Melbourne's premiership. Never deeply attached to politics or to the premiership, he found the supervision of the Queen's political education and day-to-day welfare a considerably more congenial task. In his frequent absences from the cabinet, Lord Russell became the preponderant influence in the ministry. With the Lords likely to offer stiff resistance to any further measures of reform, and an appeal to the country likely further to reduce Whig strength, as the General Election of 1837 had done, even Russell had grown more cautious about reform. The liberals and radicals in the Commons grew disillusioned and restive. When, in 1839, Melbourne suspended the Jamaican constitution, even though the reason — the resistance of planters to some features of the scheme for the abolition of slavery — was an unimpeachably liberal one, many of them objected to so autocratic a response. Melbourne's majority sank to five, and he resigned.

The resignation was provoked as much by Melbourne's boredom as by necessity, for when Peel's attempt to form a new administration foundered on the Queen's adamant refusal to change (as was customary) her ladies of the bedchamber along with her ministers, Melbourne agreed to return to the premiership and limped on for two more tedious years. Palmerston, as foreign secretary, provoked a crisis in relations with France, as well as the irritation of the radicals, as he defended Turkish despotism against the French-backed Egyptian pasha, Mehmet Ali. The government's response to the upswell of proletarian dissent associated with the onset of industrial depression in 1837 was neither firm nor sensitive. A late conversion to the radical demand for tariff reform, in particular the repeal of the Corn Laws, failed to save it. Weakened by defections and by-election defeats, the government was defeated in the Commons in June 1841 on a motion of confidence. In the General Election which followed, the party was convincingly defeated, and in August Melbourne resigned.

For a time Melbourne's close friendship with the Queen troubled his successor; but in October 1842 a stroke effectively ended his involvement in politics. Melbourne died in 1848, remembered as much for scandal as for his premiership – his marriage ended in separation in 1825, and his relationship with Caroline Norton was dragged through the divorce court in 1836. If Melbourne was the founder of the Victorian liberal party it was more by accident than design: he had little enthusiasm for reform and not much appetite for politics; and his alliance with the Irish and the radicals in 1835 was for him not much more than a marriage of convenience. Melbourne's air of nonchalance, the style of the world-weary aristocrat, was not entirely compensated for by his obvious charm. Not only was he unable to commit himself to any particular policy; he appeared to think it unnecessary to do so. His achievement was not really a political, but a pedagogic one – the gentle introduction of the inexperienced Queen into her role and responsibilities.

Sir Robert Peel
1788 – 1850

Robert Peel was born in 1788, the son of Sir Robert Peel, a wealthy Lancashire cotton manufacturer and Ellen Yates, the daughter of one of his partners. He was educated at Harrow and Christ Church, Oxford. Entering the House of Commons in 1809 for an Irish seat, Lord Liverpool, then Secretary of State for War and the Colonies, picked him as his Under-Secretary; when he became Premier, Liverpool promoted the twenty-four year old Peel to the chief Secretaryship for Ireland. Firmly opposed to Catholic emancipation – 'Orange Peel' was his inevitable nickname – he was responsible for the suppression of the Catholic Board in 1814, gaining him the lasting hostility of its leader, Daniel O'Connell; his stance helped to win him election as the member for the 'Protestant' University of Oxford in 1817. He left Ireland with the then Lord Lieutenant in 1818, and relaxed into an administrative retirement of three years.

He spent it getting married, to Julia, the daughter of General Sir John Floyd; and chairing the Commons Committee which recommended a return to the Gold standard.

He returned to Liverpool's government, as Home Secretary, in 1822. At the Home Office he undertook a thorough consolidation and reform of the criminal law, although it was not until his second spell as Home Secretary in 1828 that he was able to match it with an improvement in the control of crime, the creation of a new metropolitan police force. The 'Peelers' or 'Bobbies' began to operate the following year. Peel was at the centre of the cabinet struggle in 1825 over Catholic emancipation; and when the pro-Catholic Canning succeeded Liverpool in 1827, he and the Duke of Wellington led the 'Protestants' out of office. A few months later they returned to power: Wellington placed Peel back in his old position, and made him Leader of the Commons.

Despite their previous attitude, the increasing strength of the Catholic Association in Ireland brought both Wellington and Peel to the conviction that it could be combated effectively only if emancipation was conceded. At Wellington's request, Peel took a leading role in the promotion of the bill for emancipation, which was passed by April 1829. Peel's *volte face* on the issue was regarded by his former 'Protestant' friends with enormous bitterness. As a point of honour, he stood for re-election for his Oxford University seat, and was defeated.

Grey's election victory of 1830 (Peel was returned for Tamworth) sent Peel into opposition. He was not absolutely opposed to parliamentary reform; but the comprehensiveness of the 1831 Bill appalled him – so much so, that he refused to have anything to do with Wellington's attempt during the so-called 'days of May' in 1832 to form a ministry which would have conceded a similar measure. The passage of the Reform Act and the election of 1833 left the Tories defeated and demoralised, almost convinced that the reformed electorate would deny them office for ever. Over the next few years Peel masterminded their revival. Melbourne's dismissal in November 1834 provided the opportunity to form a government, although with the Tories so heavily outnumbered in the Commons, the ministry which Peel agreed to lead had no expectations of long survival; a

General Election was regarded as inevitable. In preparation for one, he drafted the 'Tamworth Manifesto', an influential statement of the ideology and objectives of the party which was coming to be known as 'Conservative'. It helped it to increase its strength in the January 1835 election by about one hundred.

It was not enough to overcome the Whig majority, and Peel resigned soon after Parliament assembled. Yet as Melbourne's government shuddered into inanition, Peel grew in stature and popularity. His attempt to form a ministry on Melbourne's resignation in 1839 ended in acrimonious farce as the Queen refused to replace any of the numerous Whigs in her royal household. Melbourne had to resume power, and tottered on until 1841, when, defeated in a vote of confidence, he dissolved Parliament. Peel's reputation helped the Conservatives to win the ensuing election by a majority of almost eighty. He took office at the end of August. From 1842 Peel combined the premiership with the post of Chancellor of the Exchequer.

Peel arrived in government at the height of the savage industrial depression of 1837-42. Depression had revived the demands for an end to agricultural protection, orchestrated by the Anti-Corn Law League but bitterly opposed by the agricultural interest, strongly represented on the Conservative benches; it had called forth the working-class protest movement known as 'Chartism'; and it had produced a severe crisis in national finance. The need to tackle the growing budget deficit had become urgent: taking the bull by the horns, Peel opted to reintroduce the unpopular income tax, abandoned in 1816. The measure was to be balanced by reductions in customs duties on many goods and (as a partial concession to the Anti-Corn Law League) a reduction in the duties on imported corn. Ireland was Peel's other main preoccupation. Jolted into action by Daniel O'Connell's briefly potent campaign for the repeal of the Act of Union, he set up a commission to inquire into the deeply emotive question of land occupation, while his willingness to come to terms with the Irish Catholic Church was signalled by a government grant to the Catholic seminary at Maynooth. The Maynooth grant, a breach in the exclusivity of the constitutional relationship between the State and the Anglican church, brought fierce denunciation from many of Peel's own party, and the troubled resignation of William Gladstone.

These two concerns were brought together by the blight which almost destroyed the potato harvest and threatened hardship in England and famine in Ireland. Peel, already intellectually convinced that the Corn Laws were no longer defensible, was spurred to call for their complete repeal, so that cheap corn could be purchased to prevent disaster. His cabinet was not persuaded; but Peel's resignation, and Russell's inability to form a government, enabled him to impose his will. In January 1846, he introduced a Corn Bill; with Liberal support, and despite the bitter and vigorous opposition of many of his own party, by June it had passed both Houses. Unable to prevent the Corn Bill, the Conservative dissidents, led by Lord George Bentinck, brought the government down by defeating the Irish Coercion Bill instead. At the end of June, Peel resigned. He had cut himself off permanently from a large section of his party; out of office, he lent his own support and that of his followers to the stumbling administration of Lord John Russell against the protectionist wing of his own party.

Much of the bitterness which his stance on the Corn Laws, and earlier on Catholic relief, had engendered was attributable to the sense of betrayal felt by those Tories who had regarded him as the pre-eminent representative of their own views. Peel admitted his inconsistency, but responded that by acting as he did he had done what seemed necessary to preserve, in the one case, the landed interest, and in the other, the union with Ireland. In his famous resignation speech of 1846 he predicted not only the odium which would be cast on him by his own party, but also the gratitude of working people. And indeed, by the time he died in June 1850, following a riding accident, he had achieved the status of popular hero, respected and mourned as a man who had sacrificed his own career to the cause of cheap bread for the poor.

Lord John Russell
1792 – 1878

Lord John Russell was born in 1792, the son of the sixth Duke of Bedford, Lord Lieutenant of Ireland in Grenville's 'Ministry of All the Talents'. He was educated at Westminster School and Edinburgh University. In 1813 he was elected to parliament for the family borough of Tavistock as a Whig. Illness forced him to resign in 1817, although he returned to the seat the following year.

The strength of Russell's commitment to parliamentary reform brought him to prominence in a party whose aristocratic leaders were largely hostile or indifferent; but his first major success came on the removal of religious disabilities. In 1828 he wrong-footed the government of the Duke of Wellington with his proposal for the repeal of the Test and Corporation Acts. When the Whigs returned to office under Earl Grey in 1830 committed to parliamentary reform, it fell to Russell to promote the successive Reform Bills in the Commons: in consequence, he achieved an enormous fame and popularity. Yet after the election of 1833, Russell's devotion to the cause of reform, in particular to the reform of the Irish Anglican Church, helped to expose the divisions within his party, and resulted in the departure of its conservative wing in 1834. After Grey's resignation, Russell's popularity among radicals in the Commons made him Melbourne's choice as the Leader of the House when the job became vacant later that year: but the King's opposition to the appointment of the pro-Irish and pro-reform Russell provoked him to dismiss the entire government.

The alliance between the Whigs, radicals and the Irish, which Melbourne and Russell rather gingerly agreed to in February 1835, defeated Sir Robert Peel and achieved the Whigs' restoration to power. In spite of the hostility of the King, Russell became Home Secretary and Leader of the Commons. From 1834 until 1838 he conducted a determined campaign (in the teeth of fierce opposition from the Lords) for the reform of Church and State in Ireland; a Bill reforming the municipal corporations was passed, but following the government's poor showing in the General Election of 1837, Russell had to abandon his proposals for the appropriation of the excess revenues of the Irish Church.

That election, which left the government often reliant on the support of the opposition against its own radical wing, marked the end of its commitment to reform. In a speech to the new Parliament, Russell forfeited his radical reputation by terming the 1832 settlement of the franchise 'final'. 'Finality Jack' in 1839 moved to become Colonial Secretary, holding the position as the government tottered on, beset by the rise of the Chartist movement and the Anti-Corn Law League. In the election of 1841 the Whigs were thoroughly beaten; Melbourne gave up the leadership the next year.

In opposition, Russell took up the cause of the reform of the Corn Laws, to which the Melbourne government had belatedly announced its conversion. Peel, however, overtook him, repealing the Corn laws with Russell's support in 1846. The schism in the Conservative party which followed forced Peel out of office, and presented Russell with the opportunity to form a government. Composed solely of the Whigs, without radical or Irish members, Russell's ministry depended for its survival on the support of Peel and his remaining loyalists. Even after its victory in the General Election of 1847, the government possessed little sense of purpose. Its principal items of legislation – such as the restriction of the working day in 1847 and the Public Health Act in 1848 – were measures promoted by government departments or by individual ministers, and not parts of a cabinet policy, the result of individual effort rather than of the government itself. Russell tried unsuccessfully to build a more coherent party around the defence of the free trade revolution of 1846, with, amongst other things, the repeal of the Navigation Acts in 1849, but Peel's followers, though regularly supporting the government, were not to be tempted into any formal alliance. Radicals pressed the government hard on the reduction of government spending and parliamentary reform: in 1848 a section of them led by Cobden formally dissociated themselves from the government. Russell tried to retain radical support by reopening the question of parliamentary reform: but the conservatives in his cabinet vetoed it. Russell's prestige sank; that of Palmerston, his Foreign Secretary and one of the most influential conservative voices in the cabinet, rocketed in 1850 with his confrontation with the autocratic Greek government over the Don Pacifico affair. It was soon obvious that Palmerston wanted Russell's job. Russell helped him to get it by his extraordinary attempt to whip up anti-catholic sentiment following the establishment of a Roman Catholic hierarchy in Britain; at a stroke he had alienated both the Irish and the radicals. In December 1851 Russell dismissed Palmerston, infuriated by the Foreign Secretary's casual recognition of Louis Napoleon's coup d'etat in France without cabinet authority. Palmerston had his revenge the following February when he ensured the government's defeat on its Militia Bill. Russell resigned.

After the Election of 1852 a conjunction of the Whigs and Peelites was formed under the leadership of Lord Aberdeen. Russell became Foreign Secretary and Leader of the House on the understanding that in due course Aberdeen would yield the premiership to him. Aberdeen never did, in part because it was no longer clear that he, rather than Palmerston, was in command of the Whigs. Russell, still pressing for parliamentary reform, which was still opposed by Palmerston, became ever more marginalised and worked himself up into a frenzy of wounded pride. He moved to the presidency of the council in June 1854; in January 1855 he resigned over the conduct of the Crimean War.

The rivalry between Palmerston and Russell – 'those two dreadful old men', the Queen called them – dominated the Liberals during the early 1850s; but in 1859 a reconciliation was engineered which amounted to a reformation of the party. When Palmerston formed a government in June, Russell insisted on holding the Foreign Secretaryship, and in 1861 he accepted a peerage, as Earl Russell.

Palmerston's death in October 1865 placed the premiership once more in Russell's hands. He was once again anxious to move on reform, but the complex configuration of his party – particularly the strength of a group of opponents of reform, the 'Cave of Adullam', and the desire of his radical supporters for immediate results – meant that the Bill that he introduced in March had little chance of success. The government was defeated on it in June, and resigned.

Since 1850 'selfish, peevish Johnny', as the Queen called him, had gained a reputation for tactlessness, destructive petulance and a monomaniacal interest in parliamentary reform. But Russell's pursuit of reform after 1832 was erratic, ineffective, and essentially rather conservative. It was the Tory government of the Earl of Derby which in 1867 took the wind out of Liberal sails by successfully promoting a Reform Bill which, in the end, was considerably more radical in effect than had been Russell's. Russell did not take office again, but lived on until 1878 alternately praising Gladstone and grumbling about him. Russell married in 1835 Abigail Lister. She died in 1838, and Russell was married again, in 1841, to Lady Frances Elliot, a marriage which, though happy enough, was often blamed for Russell's huffy behaviour afterwards.

The Earl of Derby
1799 – 1869

Edward George Geoffrey Smith Stanley, fourteenth Earl of Derby, was born in 1799, the son of the thirteenth earl and the heir to one of the oldest titles and greatest estates in the country. He was educated at Eton and Christ Church, Oxford, and entered Parliament as member for Stockbridge in 1820. In 1825 he married Emma, daughter of Edward Bootle Wilbraham (later Lord Skelmersdale). He described himself as 'an old constitutional Whig', although (indicating how broadly the term could by now be applied) he accepted office under Canning, and also, in 1830, from Grey, as Chief Secretary for Ireland. The position, as well as his strong High Church sympathies, placed him at the centre of the controversy over the reform of the Irish Anglican Church: his insistence that its revenues should not be appropriated to secular purposes brought about his resignation, along with a little bunch of followers known as the 'Derby Dilly', in May 1834.

Stanley's resignation marked the beginnings of his drift towards the Tory party. Courted by Peel, Stanley was not yet ready for a formal alliance in his government of 1834-5, largely because of the involvement in it of Wellington, the reformers' bête noir. But the relationship became ever closer, and on Peel's return to power in 1841, Stanley accepted the post of Colonial Secretary. The relationship between the two men was never easy, and Stanley's decision to move to the Lords in 1844 under his father's English title may have been prompted by irritation at working under Peel in the Commons. The two finally parted company over Peel's conversion to the repeal of the Corn Laws in 1845: Stanley regarded agricultural protection as central to the survival of the influence and position of the landed classes. Although he declined to form a government on Peel's resignation at the end of the year, he did not return to the reinstated Peel ministry, which accomplished repeal. As the conservatives fell into schism, Stanley became the unwilling leader of its larger, protectionist wing, even though he played little part in the debates on the Corn Bill in Parliament. Most of the party's talent had remained with Peel, and Stanley was left with a party which had numerical strength in the Commons, but no natural leaders. When Lord George Bentinck gave up its leadership in 1847 his place eventually fell to Disraeli, but it was against Stanley's will, and against the real wishes of many of the party.

On the final collapse of Russell's government in February 1852 Stanley (now Earl of Derby) formed a ministry whose weakness in the Commons, and failure to attract the support of the more conservative Whigs, left it with little option but to try its fortune at the polls. During the General Election the party deliberately played down the issue of protection, and following their modest gains dropped it altogether. Its successes were insufficient to keep it in power, and the government was forced to resign in December. To the disgust of Disraeli and the party rank-and-file, Derby turned down the opportunity of office in 1855 on the collapse of the government of Lord Aberdeen. By 1858 the Conservative party was weaker, having lost seats in the General Election of 1857, but when, on Palmerston's fall, there came a second chance to form a government, Derby took it readily. In an attempt to raise the electoral fortunes of the Conservatives by donning Liberal clothes and – to the shock of many Tories – proposing a measure of parliamentary reform, albeit a partial and partisan one. The government was inevitably defeated on the issue in the Commons, and dissolved Parliament. In the General Election which followed, the Conservatives won their best result since 1841, but it was still not enough to overcome the Whigs. In June 1859 Derby's government resigned and was replaced by Palmerston's. Palmerston's conservatism was acceptable enough to most Tories in any case, and for much of the 1859–65 parliament, Derby supported the government against its radical wing.

Palmerston's death, and a growing sense of the inevitability of parliamentary reform, shattered the political quiet of the early 1860s. Russell's defeat over reform and his resignation in July 1866 left Derby leading a minority government for the third time. Parliamentary reform now seemed to be the only way to achieve the electoral breakthrough needed to lift the Conservative party into a more secure tenure of power. Forced at first by cabinet dissent to introduce a moderate measure – against the bolder instincts of both Derby and Disraeli – the discovery that opinion in the party at large was more friendly to reform than they had guessed permitted them to face down the opposition in cabinet and to insist on a radical bill; concessions made in the course of its progress to the liberals and the radicals further widened its terms. In August 1867 the scheme received the royal assent.

By then, Derby had become very feeble; he retired a few months later, leaving the party in Disraeli's hands. Racing, rather than politics, formed the greatest interest in Derby's life (though he was also a talented classical scholar). He had been a doubtful reformer: the 1867 Act was, he said, a 'leap in the dark'. The purpose of reform, for an 'old constitutional Whig' like Derby, was not democratic politics, but to strengthen aristocratic government; and Derby, with his arrogant manner and his racehorses was nothing if not the grandest of aristocrats. Lord Derby died in 1869.

The Earl of Aberdeen
1784 – 1860

George Hamilton Gordon, fourth Earl of Aberdeen was born in 1784, the son of Lord Haddo, the heir to the third Earl. After the early death of his parents, he was adopted by William Pitt and Henry Dundas, Lord Melville; the two became his legal guardians. He was educated at Harrow and St John's College Cambridge. In 1801 he succeeded his grandfather, the Earl of Aberdeen, and spent much of the next few years on the continent, meeting Napoleon in Paris, and mounting a large archaeological dig in Athens. Pitt's death and Mclville's disgrace, both in 1806, mortified the young Aberdeen and removed his powerful patrons. That year, he was elected a Scottish representative peer, and attached himself to the remnants of Pitt's former following. But Aberdeen's attempts to break into political life seemed curiously half-hearted; he turned down a series of diplomatic posts, and although he accepted Castlereagh's request that he serve as ambassador extraordinary to Vienna in 1813, and was created Viscount Gordon of Aberdeen (in the United Kingdom peerage) for it in 1814, for a number of years afterwards he took little part in politics, occupying himself with farming and antiquarian pursuits. In 1828, however, Wellington brought him into his cabinet as Chancellor of the Duchy of Lancaster. Following the resignation of the Canningites in May, he was promoted to Foreign Secretary. He held it for no longer than Wellington did the premiership, but he returned to it in Peel's second administration in 1841.

Aberdeen's spell at the Foreign Office was inevitably compared, to its disadvantage, with the grander vision of foreign policy offered by Palmerston in his long stint of (nearly) 1830–41; yet Aberdeen after 1841 was instrumental in pulling relations with France back from the brink of war, where Palmerston had left them – although the guarantees he later received from the French minister Guizot over France's dynastic intentions in Spain later proved worthless.

Aberdeen was one of Peel's strongest supporters, and on Peel's death he became the acknowledged leader of the remnants of the Peelite party. In the confused political scene after the 1852 General Election, in which Derby's Conservative party gained seats but had not done well enough to dominate the Commons, the Peelites, in effect, held the balance of power. Aberdeen was asked to form an administration which linked the Peelites to the Whigs, and in doing so took an important step in the process by which Peel's followers, including Gladstone, became attached to the Liberal party. With Russell as its Foreign Secretary (although he was replaced by the Earl of Clarendon in early 1853), Palmerston Home Secretary, and Gladstone as Chancellor of the Exchequer, the ministry wanted neither ability nor prestige, but its effectiveness was ruined by the feud between Russell and Palmerston over the leadership of the Whig party which came to a head over Russell's Reform Bill in late 1853.

It was ironic that it was the pacific Aberdeen who should finally have become embroiled in the war against Russia in the Crimea in 1854, and it was in fact against his will that the cabinet decided to take actions which led it into the Russo-Turkish conflict. Having drifted into war, Britain was badly prepared to wage it: the stories of disorganisation and suffering which reached the public from the front produced an outcry, which wrecked what small portion of morale the government had left. In January 1855 Lord John Russell resigned, blaming his colleagues for the conduct of the war; shortly afterwards, after the government's defeat on a motion for the appointment of a select committee to inquire into the conduct of the war, Aberdeen himself resigned as well.

By the time of his resignation Aberdeen had become deeply depressed at the outbreak of the war; beset by a mysterious illness – 'perpetual noise and confusion in the head', as Gladstone described it – he had tended to the morose ever since the death of his first wife, Lady Catherine Hamilton, the daughter of the first Marquess of Abercorn, whom he had married in 1805. He married again, in 1815, Harriet Douglas, the widow of Viscount Hamilton. Aberdeen's ministry had been doomed from the start, not simply because it was a coalition, but because the Whigs within it were themselves a coalition, bitterly divided between conservatives and radicals, and between the two prima donnas, Palmerston and Russell. Aberdeen, the liberal Scottish aristocrat, was one of the few Peelites who could have attracted the alliance of the Whigs; but neither his talents nor his experience were great enough to keep the Whigs themselves allied. Lord Aberdeen died in 1860.

The Viscount Palmerston
1784 – 1865

Henry John Temple, third Viscount Palmerston was born in 1784, the eldest son of the second Viscount. For most of his first ten years he lived abroad, but returning in 1794, he was educated at Harrow, Edinburgh University and St John's College, Cambridge. He succeeded to his father's Irish peerage in 1802, and in 1807 accepted a junior post in Portland's government and secured election (eventually for Newport, Isle of Wight) to the House of Commons. In 1809 Perceval gave him the junior post of Secretary at War. There he was stuck, for almost twenty years and five administrations, gaining a reputation for bureaucratic efficiency, a hedonistic and expensive social life and a liaison with Lady Cowper (the sister of Lord Melbourne), whom he eventually married after Lord Cowper's death in 1839.

Politically, Palmerston's orientation was still rather muddled: working in a

Tory administration, and apparently content with its policies, his social connections were rather with the Whigs. He became associated with Canning (not least in his support for Catholic emancipation), who at last took him into the cabinet in 1827. After Canning's death, Palmerston, along with Melbourne, uneasily accepted office from the hands of the Duke of Wellington, but resigned in 1828, formally over the disenfranchisement of East Retford.

Palmerston's criticism of Wellington's illiberal foreign policy distanced him further from the Tories. With many of the other Canningites he was welcomed in 1830 into the Whig government of Earl Grey, even though he was doubtful about Grey's reform proposals. Palmerston was appointed Foreign Secretary, a post he was to hold almost continuously for the next eleven years. Palmerston's rather naive liberalism quickly wore off: ruthlessly and pragmatically, he pursued British interests. He built up a formidable reputation as a diplomat, achieving some remarkable successes (notably French and Dutch acceptance of Belgian independence in 1832) on the strength of little more than bluff. Palmerston presided over the period of uneasy Anglo-French cooperation which followed the French Revolution of 1830; his Quadruple Alliance of 1834 between France, Britain, Spain and Portugal was formally intended to guarantee the constitutional succession in the two latter countries, but it had as a broader aim the establishment of a western block which could act as a counterweight to the 1833 alliance of the Eastern Powers, Austria, Prussia and Russia. But the collapse of the Ottoman empire under the pressure of the ambition of the Egyptian pasha, Mehmet Ali, both forced Palmerston to accept an alliance with the Eastern powers, and revived Anglo-French competition in the Eastern Mediterranean. Palmerston's famously provocative diplomacy inflamed French anger over the issue, and in early 1840 relations with France were at their lowest ebb since the end of the Napoleonic Wars.

The fall of Melbourne in 1841 pushed Palmerston out of government. He was furious at his loss of office, and regarded his successor, Lord Aberdeen, as little short of contemptible. The Russell government of 1846-52 gave him another turn at the Foreign Office. It was during this second period that Palmerston established his liberal credentials with his party – although at the price of alienating the Queen – as he came to appear the firm supporter of the nationalist movements of 1848. When Palmerston absurdly used force in an attempt to secure compensation for the injuries suffered by two British subjects at the hands of the Greek government – the Don Pacifico affair – conservatives mounted a furious attack on his whole conduct of foreign policy: but Palmerston, displaying his now assured command of his party, vindicated himself with a speech of shamelessly rhetorical patriotism.

Palmerston may have recovered his reputation with his party, but his arrogance and independence made him an awkward colleague. His recognition of the Bonapartist coup in 1851, unauthorised by the cabinet, provoked Russell into his dismissal. A few weeks later Palmerston had his 'tit for tat with John Russell', joining the Tories to defeat the government's Militia Bill, and propelled him out of office.

Despite his contempt for Aberdeen, and what was by now a feud with Russell, Palmerston accepted office in the coalition headed by the two of them at the end of 1852, as Home Secretary. But with the development of the Crimean crisis, Palmerston's exasperation grew with Aberdeen's failure to make a clear stand against Russia. The ministry was brought down by the evidence of failures in the conduct of the war, for which he was no less responsible than any other member of the cabinet; but the popular confidence in Palmerston made him, as he called himself, 'l'inévitable'.

Coming, albeit reluctantly, to a similar conclusion, the Queen permitted Palmerston to form a government. Faced with the opposition not only of the Conservatives, but also the hostility of Russell and (after they resigned from the government over the appointment of a committee of inquiry into the conduct of the war) the remaining followers of Peel, it was weak in the Commons; but Palmerston – falling on his feet as usual – arrived in office with the Crimean war virtually won: Peace was concluded in March 1856, though rather more favourably to Russia than the Prime Minister had hoped. William Gladstone's campaign against the morality of British policy against China brought defeat in the Commons in 1857, but on appealing to the country, Palmerston won a considerably increased majority. When, though, in February 1858, he bowed to French demands for a strengthening of the conspiracy laws to prevent the harbouring of revolutionaries, Palmerston had seriously (and unusually) misinterpreted the temper of public opinion. He was defeated in the House of Commons on the measure and resigned.

Liberal disarray in opposition made essential the reconciliation of Palmerston and Russell and the alliance of old Whigs, radicals and Peelites (and particularly their star, Gladstone) an event generally regarded as the refoundation of the Victorian Liberal party. The understanding they arrived at in the course of that year enabled Palmerston to return to government despite the Conservative gains in the election of 1859, and to preside over a period of remarkable political calm. Palmerston's domestic conservatism was broadly acceptable to Lord Derby and his party; and although Palmerston continued to pay lip service to the cause of reform, there was little public pressure to drag it out again into the limelight. Almost the only source of domestic conflict lay in Gladstone's opposition, from the Treasury, to Palmerston's campaign for rearmament.

Palmerston died, over eighty, in October 1865, after victory in the general election of July. In some ways, his death was opportune: the revival of the pressure for reform, the establishment of Gladstone as the new force within the Liberal party, all indicated that Palmerston's distaste for democratic politics was no longer a practical prejudice for Liberal leaders. Palmerston had been able to stimulate and capitalise on a mood of confidence and security, and a sense – vindicated for many in the Don Pacifico affair – of the justness of British policy and the effectiveness of the *Pax Britannica*.

Benjamin Disraeli
1804 – 1881

Benjamin Disraeli was born in 1804, the son of the Jewish writer Isaac D'Israeli. Educated privately, he was received into the Church of England at the age of twelve. Disraeli attracted attention as a curious exotic. He was determined to make a name for himself through journalism, but his foray into publishing ended in failure and a nervous breakdown. A tour abroad and some literary success helped to restore him; marriage to a rich widow, Mrs Wyndham Lewis, in 1839, gave him financial stability.

Giving up his early stance as a radical independent, Disraeli entered Parliament in 1837, for Maidstone, as a Tory. Rebuffed in his requests for office by Peel, Disraeli began to create, with a few friends, a party within the Tories. 'Young England' had little lasting political impact; but it helped to form Disraeli's views. His most famous novels, *Coningsby* of 1844 and *Sybil* of 1845 epitomised these, a lament for the social consequences of England's rapid industrialisation accompanied by a distaste for the post-1688 Whiggish oligarchy and a romantic nostalgia for the paternalism and royalism of the seventeenth-century Tories.

By 1845 Disraeli was in open rebellion against Peel; in 1846 he was rhetorically the most brilliant of the Conservatives who fought the Corn Bill tooth and nail through the Commons. After the secession of the Peelites, he was one of the few stars among the Tory protectionists, but racial and social snobbery excluded him from any formal role until 1848, when Lord George Bentinck's death left the party without a leader in the Commons, and Disraeli's purchase of a country estate made him more acceptable. When in 1852 Lord Derby briefly formed a minority Conservative administration, Disraeli became Chancellor of the Exchequer, and before the government left office in December, put together a budget which signalled the party's move away from protection. Once it had abandoned protection, however, Derby's party was left with little to differentiate itself from the Whiggish governments of Palmerston and Aberdeen.

To Disraeli's disgust, Derby turned down the chance of forming a ministry on the collapse of Aberdeen's government. Not until 1858 was there a second chance, when Palmerston, for once misjudging the political mood, was defeated on his Conspiracy to Murder Bill. This time Derby took it up. The government was, again, a minority one, and lived only briefly; but its conversion to parliamentary reform, although partial and partisan, recast the Conservative party as the party of 'Conservative progress', and it reaped the benefits (though not sufficiently to retain power) in the General Election later the same year.

The election of 1859 proved a false dawn, as the country settled down under Palmerston to a period of contented and largely passionless politics. The election of 1865 reversed the Tory gains of 1859; but Palmerston's death, later the same year, gave the Conservatives their chance to seize the political initiative. Lord Russell's failure to sort out the divisions in his own party over parliamentary reform, and his resignation in June 1866, brought Derby and Disraeli back into power. Though initially uncommitted to reform, the government came quickly to recognise its attraction as a means of reversing the Conservatives' electoral decline, as well as to avoid a Liberal settlement of the question which might entrench them in power for the next few decades. Counting on splitting the Liberals and gaining the support of the radicals, Derby and Disraeli introduced a bold measure, facing down cabinet resignations and imperturbably accepting many of the radical amendments which were proposed to it. By reducing the Liberals to confusion, Disraeli won the acclaim of his party, as well as, on Derby's retirement in 1868, its leadership.

Disraeli's achievement looked less impressive after the election of 1868 had returned Gladstone and the Liberals to power. In 1872 the Tory grandees were on the verge of pushing him out, while the death of his wife the same year drove him close to despair. But the strains of reform had also, by 1873, ruined the Liberals, and when Gladstone finally called a general election in February 1874 the Conservatives – to universal surprise, and for the first time in more than thirty years – won an overall majority.

Partly through unpreparedness, and partly through choice, Disraeli came to power with little in the way of a set of policies, although in two speeches in 1872 he had identified the party with the defence of the empire and social reform. But by 1875, as Gladstone retired from the leadership of the Liberals, and with Disraeli completely in command of the Commons, he had embarked on an impressive programme of social and industrial reform, including, remarkably, extensions to the right of trade union combination and legislation on public health and housing. Thereafter the government's activity slowed. Disraeli retired from the Commons in 1876, accepting a peerage as Earl of Beaconsfield, just as the government became increasingly preoccupied with foreign affairs. The savagery of the response of the crumbling Turkish regime to Christian revolts in the Balkans in 1876 produced a wave of revulsion – ably capitalised upon by Gladstone – for Britain's support for the Eastern despotism; while Russia looked set to intervene, Disraeli's cabinet became bitterly divided over the extent to which Turkey should be defended. Despite his failure to protect Turkey in the war which followed, Beaconsfield in the end came out of the affair with credit, forcing Russia to the Congress of Berlin in 1878 without declaring war.

Beaconsfield's rhetorical attachment to the idea of empire was marked in his Act making the Queen Empress of India; but imperial expansion, with the Afghan mission of 1878-80 and the war against the Zulus of 1878-9, happened largely without the prior approval of the government and against its instincts – and also produced some bloody reverses. These, an agricultural depression, and simply the government's failure to make any strong impression on the minds of voters left it an easy target for Gladstone's Midlothian campaign in the General Election of 1880.

Not long after the defeat, in 1881, Beaconsfield died. Disraeli was a charmer, whose dandyism attracted some (among them Queen Victoria, who thought him 'full of poetry, romance and chivalry'), but repelled many of the rather more hearty figures within the Tory party. An outsider in the Tory party, he had formed a romantic and reactionary view of it and the society it defended. But beneath the rhetoric he was a realist, an opportunist and a party loyalist, happy to sacrifice intellectual consistency to party advantage.

William Gladstone
1809 – 1898

William Ewart Gladstone was born in Liverpool in 1809, the son of Sir John Gladstone, a successful Liverpool businessman, Canningite and evangelical. He was educated at Eton and Christ Church, Oxford. His precocity and his ardent Toryism – at Oxford he led a campaign against the Reform Bill of 1832 – took him into the House of Commons in December 1832, despite a profound piety which led him for a while to toy with the idea of joining the priesthood.

Peel gave him junior office, and his patronage. By 1841 he was Vice-President of the Board of Trade, responsible for much of the detail of Peel's tariff reform proposals; in 1843 he became President. Delighting in the technical detail of his department, Gladstone gradually came to view the cause of free trade with an almost religious zeal – the more so, because his youthful belief in the role of an allied Church and State as the defender of the nation's identity and the agent of its moral development had begun to succumb to reality. The crunch in his relationship with High Anglicanism came with Peel's proposal for state funding of the Irish Catholic seminary at Maynooth: Gladstone felt compelled to resign from the government, as was consistent with his earlier principles; but unable to deny its practical benefits, as a private member he supported the idea. The crisis in Peel's government caused by his decision to repeal the Corn Laws brought Gladstone, a firm supporter of the plan, back to office as Secretary of State for the Colonies. He resigned with Peel in 1846, and found himself divided from the main, protectionist, body of his party. On Peel's death, Gladstone effectively inherited the leadership of the small rump of Peelites in the Commons.

Courted by both Liberals and Conservatives, Gladstone and the Peelites wavered between them. In 1852, Gladstone's demolition of Disraeli's budget was to help bring down the government of Derby, and in the coalition of Whigs, Peelites and radicals under Lord Aberdeen which replaced it, Gladstone was Chancellor of the Exchequer. His first budget, in April 1853, was a fiscal and oratorical triumph: he reformed the income tax and envisaged its eventual abolition, and in doing so was established both as a safe Chancellor and as a dominant figure in the Commons. Gladstone and many of the Peelites resigned shortly after Aberdeen did, in early 1855, as a protest against Palmerston's acceptance of a committee of inquiry into the conduct of the Crimean War. In opposition once more, Gladstone continued to waver between Liberals and Conservatives: distrust of Palmerston, and a residual affection tempted him towards the Conservatives; but doubts about their protectionist instincts, as well as dislike of Disraeli, impelled him towards the Liberals. In 1858 he took a decisive choice, turning down Derby's offer of a post in his Conservative administration; in 1859 he joined Palmerston's government, again as Chancellor.

The relationship between the two men was never an easy one: Gladstone fought a long battle with Palmerston over the government's programme of rearmament, in which his desire for economy mingled with disapproval of the Prime Minister's pandering to the rawest nationalistic emotions of the people. Government expenditure forced the retention of the income tax, although this allowed him to continue his steady removal of customs and excise duties. By abolishing one of the duties – the excise duty on paper – Gladstone satisfied one radical demand and provoked (and overcame) a confrontation with the Lords. Gladstone was, in fact, moving towards a more radical Liberalism; but his interest in reform in the 1860s was based only secondarily on a belief in the justice of the wider suffrage. The existing franchise, he thought, permitted Parliament to be used and abused by sectional interests; by the creation of a wider political constituency, Gladstone hoped to create a more virtuous politics. Gladstone's methods had rather more radical implications. Through a series of public speeches in the provinces, Gladstone established himself as the popular candidate for succession to Palmerston – the 'People's William'. His defeat at Oxford University in 1865 and his subsequent success at South Lancashire strengthened the image. In fact it was Russell who took the premiership on the death of Palmerston. He and Gladstone designed the moderate, but unsuccessful, Reform Bill of 1866, whose defeat brought the Conservatives back into power. Derby and Disraeli trumped the Liberal reform plans with their own, in the event, more radical measure. Gladstone may have been discomforted, but he was still seen in the country at large as the champion of reform: the success of the Liberals at the General election of 1868 was attributable to his popularity; and (since Russell had resigned in December 1867) Gladstone became leader of his first government.

Gladstone is said to have responded to the message bringing the news that he would be asked to form a government with the words 'my mission is to pacify Ireland'. The rise of Fenianism had placed the country firmly back on the British political agenda by the late 1860s; and Gladstone had already identified the disestablishment of the Irish Church as a great Liberal preoccupation, showing how far he had come since his opposition to the appropriation of the Irish Church revenues in the 1830s. His Irish Church Bill received Royal Assent in July 1869. His attempts also to create a state-supported, non-denominational ministry brought about the government's defeat in 1873, and Gladstone's resignation – which was rescinded when Disraeli, unprepared for office, turned down the opportunity to form a government. The other plank of Gladstone's effort to pacify Ireland – the Irish Land Bill – was approached with greater circumspection. The distinctly moderate Act passed in 1870 did create greater security from eviction and rent increases for Irish tenants and provoked alarm among landowners, but it failed to satisfy Irish demands.

The widely ranging domestic reforms of Gladstone's first administration were largely the work of others: he played little part in the passage of W.E. Forster's great Education Act of 1870; nor in that of the Trade Union reforms of 1871; nor in Cardwell's abolition of the purchase of army commissions – though he saw it as a welcome blow for efficiency against privilege. Never particularly disciplined, the party's unity wasted away after the great bills of 1869-70; the decline of the effectiveness of the Liberals in Parliament was matched by the decline of Liberal enthusiasm in the constituencies, and a certain resentment of Gladstone's dominance. Gladstone called an early election in 1874: unable to unite his party on anything else, he determined to offer the country rigidly economical government and the abolition of the income tax. The result reversed the Liberal victory of 1874: Disraeli came to power and stayed until 1880.

In 1875 Gladstone resigned as leader of the Liberal party, and for the next two years returned to his central concern, the role of the Church, devoting much of his time to a rebuttal of the 1870 Vatican Council decree on papal infallibility, which had ruined the prospects for English ecumenism and called into question the secular allegiance of all Roman Catholics. He was called back to secular concerns by the outcry over the Turkish atrocities in Bulgaria in 1876. Taking up a moral crusade against what he saw as the cynicism and immorality of Disraeli's refusal to intervene, his stance caught the public imagination, and broadened after 1878 into a more general denunciation of the Conservatives' foreign policy. 'Beaconsfieldism' – as Gladstone called it – was seen as unjust, incompetent, and liable to corrupt. Gladstone's energetic campaign in Midlothian before and during the election of 1880 confirmed his moral authority within the party which virtually dictated that he be summoned to form a Liberal government after its convincing victory.

Gladstone came to power in 1880 without a programme, but determined to reverse 'Beaconsfieldism'. Turkey was put firmly in its place, and British forces were withdrawn from much of Afghanistan. Retreating from empire in Africa proved more complicated. Gladstone's delay in addressing Boer demands for self-government led to the South African rebellion in 1881 and the government's rather muddled creation of a half-way house to independence in the Convention of Pretoria. Most seriously, Gladstone could only respond to the Egyptian nationalist revolt of 1881 with the bombardment of Alexandria and the occupation of Egypt. To the horror of radicals, the Liberal party appeared not only to be acting in much the same way as Disraeli had, but to be doing so much worse. Confidence was not improved by the botched handling of the Sudanese rising which resulted in the massacre of General Gordon in 1885.   .

But the major preoccupation of the 1880s was again Ireland: the foundation of the Irish Land League in 1879, the strength of the Home Rule party of Charles Stewart Parnell, and the effectiveness of its disruption of the Commons forced the government to take action. The Irish Land Act of 1881 made the concessions on the rights of tenants which had been withheld in 1870; but at the same time mounting unrest forced the government reluctantly to introduce emergency measures in the same year. Their obstruction by the Parnellites produced a procedural revolution in the Commons. As Irish fenian 'outrages' grew in number, the government sought to come to terms with Parnell; but the 'Phoenix Park murders' of the Chief Secretary and Under-Secretary for Ireland hardened hearts in the cabinet, to Gladstone's own distress.

The radicals within the Liberal party continued to press for further measures of parliamentary reform. In 1884 time was found for a Bill extending the franchise; ultimately it was forced through only by dint of a deal with the Conservatives which added to it a redistribution of seats.

Gladstone's government finally went off the rails in June 1885, after it was defeated on the budget. The General Election held later that year resulted in a curious situation: the strength of the Conservatives and Parnellites exactly equalled that of the Liberals. Lord Salisbury became head of a minority Conservative government. Gladstone had already been moving towards a Home Rule solution for Ireland; his conviction that Salisbury would fail to settle the country left him resolved on it. Engineering the government's defeat, he returned to power and shocked his party by bringing forward a Home Rule Bill in April 1886. It split the Liberals: the old Whig Lord Hartington and the imperialist radical Joseph Chamberlain left Gladstone and the party and helped defeat the Bill on its second reading. Gladstone placed his Home Rule proposal before the electorate, and lost. Hartington and Chamberlain and their Liberal Unionist party had come to an understanding with the Conservatives, aiding them to take office again.

Gladstone was beginning to lose his hold over even the mainstream of the Liberal party. What was now almost an obsession with Home Rule was shared by few of his colleagues, who cast around for a wider programme. The Liberals returned to power in the election of 1892, depending on the Irish for support against the Conservatives and Unionists. Gladstone's priority, the Home Rule Bill, was, with a certain inevitability, thrown out by the Lords in 1893. Gladstone's last ministry was rent by squabbles and marred by the Prime Minister's isolation from much of his cabinet. Exhausted and finally at odds with the rest of the government over his opposition to increased spending on the naval estimates, Gladstone resigned in March 1894.

Gladstone had married in 1839 Catherine, the daughter of Sir Stephen Glynne, through whom he came to possess Hawarden Castle. The marriage was a very close and affectionate one; but Gladstone was tortured by his fascination with women, which he both relieved and irritated with his work with the redemption of prostitutes, to the alarm of his colleagues. Even after his retirement at eighty-four, Gladstone continued to write and agitate – on ecumenism, and on the Turks' oppression of the Armenians. Phenomenally pious and learned, his intellectual and moral authority – however alienating the first and irritating the second were – made him tower above his colleagues and his opponents. By the time of his death the Liberal party had largely grown out of his shadow, moving away from his preoccupations of Ireland, religion and cheap government. His leadership had in any case been at times nominal: he had inspired, rather than managed the party, and held it together largely because of his success in balancing the views of both Whigs and radicals. He died in 1898.

The Marquess of Salisbury
1830 – 1903

Robert Arthur Talbot Gascoyne-Cecil, third Marquess of Salisbury, was born in 1830, the son of the second Marquess who had held cabinet office in the Conservative governments of 1852 and 1858. He was educated at Eton and Christ Church, Oxford, and in 1853 was elected to Parliament at Stamford, as a Conservative. Already a prolific journalist, his writing helped to support him following his father's disapproval of his marriage in 1857 to Georgina, the daughter of Sir Edward Hall Alderson. His articles for the Tory *Quarterly Review* made his reputation as a conservative thinker, unstinting in his attacks on the abandonment of the party's principles for expediency which he believed Disraeli's leadership of the party represented, and deeply concerned with the threat to the propertied and the educated from the march of democracy, with the defence of the Church against the assaults of radicals and dissenters, and with the preservation of European order against the march of nationalism.

Despite his attacks on the party leadership, Viscount Cranborne (as he had now become) was appointed to the Indian Secretaryship in the Derby government. But while he came to appreciate the advantages of the Conservatives pre-empting Liberal parliamentary reform, he was unable to accept Disraeli's radical plan for household suffrage without greater safeguards, and in February 1867 he left the cabinet.

On the death of his father early the next year, the new Marquess of Salisbury moved to the House of Lords. Bored by the peers and demoralised by the Reform Act, he retreated for a while to his chapel and laboratory in Hatfield, gloomily contemplating the destruction of aristocratic government and a new era of class warfare.

Salisbury, with his ally Lord Carnarvon, consented to enter the government on Disraeli's election victory of 1874, still unreconciled to the Prime Minister, but preferring to keep an eye on him from inside the ministry. The Prime Minister continued to appal him, and Salisbury contemplated resignation over his support for the Public Worship Regulation Bill, a measure aimed against Anglican high churchmanship. Salisbury had taken the India Office in 1874; but he was soon embroiled in the Bulgarian crisis. On the resignation of Derby, the Foreign Secretary, in 1878, Beaconsfield (as Disraeli had now become) chose Salisbury to replace him. Confronting Russia over its intervention in the Balkans, Beaconsfield and Salisbury recovered some credit from the whole Bulgarian affair, cementing 'peace with honour', as they called it, at the Congress of Berlin in 1878.

Salisbury's success, and popular appreciation of it, converted him into a candidate for the succession to Beaconsfield. The Conservatives lost the General Election of 1880, and Beaconsfield died a year later. For the next few years the party leadership was rather unhappily shared between Sir Stafford Northcote and Salisbury. Salisbury's handling of the negotiations with Gladstone over the franchise and redistribution bills in 1884, as well as Lord Randolph Churchill's attacks on Northcote, enhanced his reputation, and on the fall of Gladstone's government in June 1885, it was Salisbury who became Prime Minister, albeit of a minority government installed only because the redistribution bill of the previous year precluded an Election before November.

The election left Parnell's Irish Home Rule party exactly holding the balance of power between Liberals and Conservatives. Salisbury had before it come to an understanding with Parnell; but the revelation of Gladstone's conversion to Home Rule helped to convert the Conservatives into an overtly Unionist party. Gladstone brought Salisbury's government down, defeating it on a bill giving emergency powers in Ireland in January 1886, and formed a government himself. He proceeded to split his own party with Home Rule, and appealed to the verdict of a General Election in July. Salisbury, in collaboration with the Liberal Unionists under Joseph Chamberlain and Lord Hartington, won a majority of 120. The implications of the relationship took time to emerge. Neither Salisbury, nor the Liberal Unionists, were too anxious to formalise it. The Prime Minister replaced his Chancellor, Lord Randolph Churchill, when it appeared that he was beginning to work closely together with Chamberlain: the ambitious and mercurial Churchill succumbed thereafter to a self-destructive diet of women and drink. Liberal Unionist support for the government was in any case unreliable on anything except Ireland. Salisbury was particularly suspicious of the pressure from Unionists for local government reform, and although he accepted the construction of the London County Council (which soon became a Liberal fief) it was a concession which he deeply resented. Salisbury was still as concerned as ever about the consequences of democratic politics. One measure he presented as radical and progressive – the establishment of free elementary schooling – had its roots rather in his concern for the future of the Church of England schools.

Salisbury's main preoccupation, however, was to be with the the balance of power in Europe and with the empire. Taking over the Foreign Office himself in 1887 Salisbury adopted a pragmatic and sceptical stance. Some called it 'splendid isolation'; but although he avoided the entanglement of formal alliances, he sought to remain warily on good terms with Germany, while he prevented either a Russian war over Bulgaria or another attack by Bismarck on France. He saw the dangers involved in imperial expansion, although he also recognised how consolidation of the Empire could help to bolster British power. He tried, but failed, to pull British troops out of Egypt; and if he presided over the efforts of imperialists to seize parts of Africa it was not because he himself possessed much of a desire to acquire territory, but because he believed it to be vital to prevent British interests from being stifled by other, rival, powers.

The General Election of 1892 returned a majority of forty for Home Rule under Gladstone, but the defeat of his Home Rule Bill and his resignation left the Liberal party confused and demoralised: in 1895 they were put out of their misery and expelled from office. Salisbury had been anxious after the Liberals' victory in 1892 to establish a more formal agreement with the Liberal Unionists, aided by the cooling of Chamberlain's enthusiasm for social reform (increasingly, he diverted his energies into colonial affairs). The Conservative–Unionist alliance took office, with a cabinet for the first time containing Chamberlain and some other Unionists. In the General Election later that year the Liberals were devastated.

Salisbury again reserved the Foreign Office to himself. His attempts to avoid confrontation abroad clashed with the bellicose imperialist ambitions of Chamberlain, now Colonial Secretary (who argued for an alliance between Britain and Germany to carve up the world between them), and ran counter to the uncontrollable impulses of buccaneers such as Cecil Rhodes. Chamberlain's attempts to pull South Africa back from its semi-independence ended in 1899 with the dispatch of an army, and the bloody Boer war.

Salisbury took advantage of popular enthusiasm for the war by calling the 'Khaki election' that year, which won the government an increased majority. But tired and ill, and eclipsed by the restless energy of Chamberlain and by his nephew Balfour, Salisbury was marginalised within the government. In 1900 his colleagues had dislodged him from the Foreign Office. In July 1902 he resigned from the Premiership.

Unflamboyant and self-effacing, Salisbury had never captured the imagination either of the public or his party. In later life he had receded from the apocalyptic dread of democracy of his early writings, but his philosophical pessimism still led him to politically unfashionable notions about the worth of reform and state intervention, and convinced him of the need to resist, or at least to limit, change. He died in August 1903.

The Earl of Rosebery
1847 – 1929

Archibald Philip Primrose, fifth Earl of Rosebery, was born in 1847, the grandson of the fourth Earl. He was educated at Eton and Christ Church, Oxford. On the death of his grandfather in 1868 (his father, Lord Dalmeny, an enthusiast for physical fitness, died of a heart attack in 1850) he succeeded to the earldom of Rosebery and the family's Scottish estates. Racing, rather than studying or politics, formed his chief interest at Oxford, and resulted in his being sent down.

Rosebery was not simply a socialite. His inheritance made him one of the greatest landowners in Scotland; and he was soon exercising his considerable influence in favour of Gladstonian Liberalism. His marriage in 1878 to Hannah de Rothschild, the heiress of the Rothschild fortune, consolidated his position in the first rank of the Scottish aristocracy. He became marked out as the future leader of the Scottish Liberals, and his assistance to Gladstone in his Midlothian campaign of 1879-80 brought him a national reputation. But Rosebery's relationship with Gladstone was an awkward one, fraught with misunderstanding. Rosebery, increasingly absorbed in the government of Scotland, accepted the post of Under-Secretary in the Home Office with special responsibility for Scottish affairs in 1881. But angered by Gladstone's neglect both of him and of Scotland, in 1883 he resigned.

During a world tour in 1883-4, Rosebery turned his mind to the development of a liberal understanding of the Empire; on his return he became chairman of the Imperial Federation League. He rejoined the government in its hour of crisis in early 1885 as Lord Privy Seal, and, after the election of that year and the brief Conservative administration, he returned with Gladstone to take the Foreign Secretaryship in the short-lived government of 1886. Amid the convulsions in the Liberal party caused by Home Rule and the aftermath of the defeat of 1886, Rosebery won the respect of Liberals, and, for a while, the approval of Gladstone. As Chairman of the new London County Council in 1889, Rosebery magnified his attraction to a younger generation of Liberals, as he became identified with urban concerns and with the constructive social policy of its dominant Progressive Party. But the death of his wife in November 1890 prompted a genuine desire to withdraw from politics; abroad for much of the following eighteen months, he played no part in the acrimonious debates on policy which preceded the 1892 Election, and was only with difficulty induced to return to the Foreign Office when Gladstone formed his cabinet after it.

Rosebery ran the Office with little reference to the rest of the cabinet, and certainly not to the Prime Minister. Gladstone determined to take British forces out of Egypt; Rosebery tried to keep them there: Gladstone and the Chancellor, Sir William Harcourt, wanted no further expansion in Africa; Rosebery quietly made preparations to make Uganda a British protectorate.

Harcourt was widely seen as Gladstone's successor. But when, on Gladstone's resignation in 1894, the Queen chose to summon the patrician Rosebery rather than the irascible Chancellor, the party in general was fairly relieved. Rosebery's premiership was brief and unhappy. He, Harcourt and John Morley (the Chief

Secretary for Ireland) would not speak to one another; he infuriated the Irish and many Liberals with his announcement that Home Rule for Ireland would have to wait until a majority of English members of parliament voted for it; and his attempt to bar French access to the Upper Nile through a treaty with Belgium brought down on his head the fury of the cabinet, France and Germany. The demoralisation of the party was complete by June 1895: defeat in the Commons gave Rosebery an opportunity, seized gratefully, to resign.

The General Election of 1895 went virtually by default. Rosebery continued as nominal leader, but when Gladstone emerged from retirement to take up the plight of the Armenian Christians the following year, he announced 'I have resigned the leadership of the Liberal Party – that is, if I ever held it, of which I am not quite sure'. But despite the debâcle of 1895, a group of Liberal Imperialists still looked to him as their head; after the battle over Liberal policy on the empire was joined in earnest over the South African war of 1899-1902, Rosebery mounted a stinging, though often obscure, attack on Campbell–Bannerman's leadership, and with Asquith and Sir Edward Grey formed a breakaway Liberal League.

The vision of an alternative Liberal party was short-lived: the League's distaste for 'faddism', its old, aristocratic Whig overtones, and its rather vague notions about 'national efficiency' struck few chords among Liberals. Rosebery's allies soon returned to the party fold, and he himself became isolated in his hostility to Campbell-Bannerman's Home Rule proposals. Finally alienated from the Liberals by what he regarded as the revolutionary and socialist budget introduced by Lloyd George in 1909, his views tended more and more to the Conservatives, and even away from politics altogether. In 1911, he was raised to the peerage of the United Kingdom as Earl of Midlothian. He died in 1929. Rosebery had charm, ability and intelligence; but his flippancy and his horseracing gave an impression of dilettantism (even to the Queen) and seemed offensive to many Liberals on the nonconformist wing of the party.

Arthur Balfour
1848 – 1930

Arthur James Balfour was born in East Lothian in 1848, the son of James Balfour MP and his wife, the sister of the third Marquess of Salisbury, later the Conservative Prime Minister. He was educated at Eton and Trinity College, Cambridge. Under the influence of Henry Sidgwick, the moral philosopher, Balfour became interested in metaphysics; donnish, delicate, and fond of polite society, Balfour seemed too effete for the rougher world of the House of Commons. His mother and her brother, however, led him into politics: Balfour became MP for Hertford in 1874, and Parliamentary Private Secretary to Salisbury, then Foreign Secretary, in 1877. Friendly with Lord Randolph Churchill since Eton, Balfour collaborated with him to embarrass Sir Stafford Northcote, the Conservative leader in the Commons, helping to ensure that Salisbury would secure command of the party in the succession struggle that followed Beaconsfield's 1880 electoral defeat.

In Salisbury's government of 1886, Balfour became briefly Secretary of State for Scotland before he was brought into the cabinet as Chief Secretary for Ireland. Given the task of carrying out the repressive programme agreed on by the cabinet in response to a terrorist campaign, he earned himself the sobriquet (from the nationalists) of 'Bloody Balfour', the approval of Conservative hardliners, and the succession to W.H. Smith as leader of the House of Commons, combined with the office of first Lord of the Treasury in October 1891. He was, in effect, the heir apparent to his uncle.

Balfour returned both to the Leadership of the Commons and to the Treasury after the intermission of the Gladstone and Rosebery administrations, the defeat of Irish Home Rule, and the landslide victory of the Conservative-Liberal Unionist alliance in 1895. Over the next few years, Balfour found himself increasingly in command of the government, though its driving force seemed often to be the Unionist leader and Colonial Secretary, Joseph Chamberlain. On the conclusion of the Boer War, in July 1902, Salisbury resigned, and Balfour formally took over as Prime Minister.

Chamberlain had recognised that his radical past, if nothing else, excluded him from leadership of the Conservatives, and his motives in embarking on an explosive personal crusade for a preferential customs tariff for the colonies in May 1903 are obscure. Chamberlain aimed with his proposal not only to cement the relationship between the mother-country and the empire, but also to keep Britain ahead in the battle for industrial supremacy with the other European powers, and raise extra money for his pet project, an old age pension scheme.

The conflict which imperial preference raised between protectionists and free-traders within the party became intense: Balfour tried, effectively, to obscure his own position and suppress the debate; but he could not prevent the cabinet clash of September 1904 which ended with the resignation of Chamberlain and four other, free-trade, ministers. Chamberlain took the debate into the constituencies with his Tariff Reform League, while Balfour tried to put it off with the suggestion of an imperial conference and elections in Britain and the colonies specifically on the issue – his 'double election' pledge. The issue was, for

Balfour, a distraction from more pressing matters. The threat of Russian encroachment on Persia and India, the growth of German naval power, and the inadequacies of the British forces in the South African War made military reform and the search for continental allies overriding concerns. Balfour aimed to improve military decision making and reform the War Office; and his alliances with the Japanese (in 1902) and the French (the *entente cordiale* of 1904) were intended to overcome the diplomatic isolation of the Salisbury years.

Tariff reform would keep on intruding, however, bringing a new crisis in May 1905 when Balfour appeared to be receding from his earlier promise on the double election. He hung on to office until December 1905, anxious to conclude the renewal of the Japanese Treaty and to entrench his defence reforms. In the General Election which followed his resignation the Conservatives were swept from power; Balfour himself was defeated at East Manchester, and had to find refuge at the City of London.

The catastrophic defeat left him only tenuously in charge of the party. Chamberlain's stroke in 1906, from which he never fully recovered, eased, a little, the pressure on him to move further towards tariff reform, and Lloyd George's 'People's Budget' of April 1909 was something against which all the Unionists could unite. But the aftermath of the struggle over the Liberals' Finance Bill was to lead to Balfour's downfall: he had warned against using the House of Lords as an absolute defence against the social reforms planned by the Liberal government, and his refusal to fight a last ditch battle against the Parliament Bill of 1911 resulted in a bitterly hostile campaign against his leadership. Late that year he resigned as the party's leader.

When war broke out in 1914, Asquith brought Balfour into the advisory Committee on Imperial Defence, now known as the War Council, as a gesture to the Conservatives; when the first Coalition government was formed in May 1915, he became First Lord of the Admiralty, the only Conservative in a senior position. Balfour supported Lloyd George's adroit putsch to take over the government from Asquith in December 1916, and was made Foreign Secretary on the formation of the new coalition. He formed a close association with the premier, although Lloyd George's personal conduct of the post-war summitry left him, at times, with little to do. The famous Balfour Declaration of 1917, committing Britain to the creation of a Jewish state in Palestine, however, won him the passionate support of world Jewry. In 1919 he resigned the Foreign Secretaryship, although he stayed on as Lord President, acting as the government's delegate to the widening circuit of international conferences.

Balfour tried to defend the coalition, and Lloyd George, when many of his Conservative colleagues revolted against them in 1922; but following their success, he resigned, along with Lloyd George. He was created Earl of Balfour and Viscount Traprain. In Baldwin's second administration of 1925 to 1929, he performed a similar role to that he had played in the last years of the Lloyd George coalition. International conferences were more attuned to Balfour's philosophical mind than was the daily aggravation of party politics; yet his mind, his charm and his style concealed a ruthless political instinct: Beatrice Webb called him 'strong-willed, swift in execution, utterly cynical, and honestly contemptuous of that pitiful myth "democracy".' An executive politician who plainly enjoyed office – cynics pointed to how he clung to it even when most other Conservatives had fled in 1922 – he was overshadowed by strong populists like Chamberlain or Lloyd George. Balfour died on 19 March 1930.

Sir Henry Campbell-Bannerman
1836 – 1908

Sir Henry Campbell-Bannerman was born in Glasgow in 1836, the son of Sir James Campbell, Lord Provost of the city and one of the founders of the drapery firm of J. and W. Campbell, and his wife Janet, the daughter of Henry Bannerman, a Manchester industrialist. Campbell-Bannerman (he became double-barrelled in 1871 on the receipt of an inheritance) was educated at Glasgow High School, Glasgow University, and Trinity College, Cambridge. In 1858 he joined his father's business. Marriage, to the invalid Charlotte, daughter of Major-General Sir Charles Bruce, in 1860, meant that he spent regular spells abroad each year, nursing her at Marienbad and other continental spas. His father, self-made, was a Tory; but Campbell-Bannerman contested, and won the Stirling burghs in 1868 as a radical Liberal.

In the governments of Gladstone, Campbell-Bannerman ascended rather slowly: in 1871-4 and in 1880-2 he was Financial Secretary to the War Office; in 1882-4 Secretary to the Admiralty; in 1884-5 Chief Secretary for Ireland. In 1886, in Gladstone's third administration, he was brought into the cabinet, as Secretary of State for War, and he returned to the post in Gladstone's fourth and last government, in 1892. Campbell-Bannerman had been a member of the Hartington Commission set up by Salisbury in 1888 to consider military reform; in office he rejected one of its principal recommendations, the establishment of an army general staff, reflecting the contemporary Liberal suspicion of militarism. His greatest achievement was to persuade the elderly and none-too-bright Commander-in-Chief of the army, the Duke of Cambridge, to retire.

Popular in the Commons for his personal, not his political, qualities, with no particular ambitions and with no particular power-base within or outside the party, Campbell-Bannerman assumed the leadership of the parliamentary party almost by default. In 1895 he had been speaking of abandoning politics to take up the vacant Speakership. But the factional war for the head and the soul of the Liberals which erupted after Rosebery's resignation propelled him to a senior position. Sir William Harcourt resigned the leadership in the Commons in 1898; John Morley withdrew thereafter; and Herbert Asquith, generally acknowledged as the party's rising star, but still relatively junior (and reluctant to lose his earnings as a barrister) deferred to the older Campbell-Bannerman. Campbell-Bannerman could, at least, be seen as taking a middling position in the current party debate between Gladstonians and imperialists, and, as such, represented a compromise. His acceptance of the position in 1899 came as a surprise to many; and to some the appointment of this second-rank figure merely showed to how parlous a state the Liberals had been reduced.

Campbell-Bannerman was soon, however, to make his own views on imperialism clearer. His denunciation of the conduct of the South African War carried with it a majority of the parliamentary party: but a minority, including Asquith, joined the Liberals' elder statesman, Rosebery, in supporting the Salisbury government. After the Liberals' crushing defeat at the election of 1900, the dispute became inflamed, among other things, by Campbell-Bannerman's June 1901 speech condemning the 'methods of barbarism' − concentration camps

– by which Kitchener was waging the war. Despite the threat of a formal schism with the creation of Rosebery's Liberal League in 1902, Rosebery and his imperialist associates failed to follow up their initiative: by 1905 Rosebery was going his own way over Irish Home Rule. Campbell-Bannerman gained a hold over the party, if only by taking a steady line; and the revival of the free-trade debate following Joseph Chamberlain's proposal of Imperial Preference in 1903 produced an unimpeachably Gladstonian issue on which all elements of the party could agree. Which is not to say that Campbell-Bannerman's leadership was yet assured: right up to his installation as Prime Minister in 1905 his 'imperialist' colleagues continued to plot against him.

Campbell-Bannerman consolidated his position as the fall of the Conservatives was eagerly anticipated with a series of speeches outlining his programme of social reform and giving a commitment to Irish self-government; and when Balfour finally resigned, in December 1905, the conspiracy against him collapsed as he appointed two of the conspirators – Asquith and Sir Edward Grey – to the Chancellorship and the Foreign Office. Calling a General Election almost immediately, Campbell-Bannerman benefited from the free-trade issue, a negative vote against the Tories, and his pact with the Labour party, which prevented, in many constituencies, a split between 'Progressive' forces. He won a landslide victory.

Though obscured by the disarray in the Conservative party, there was still confusion and incoherence in the Liberal ranks, in particular over the extent to which it should seek to identify itself with working-class interests. Campbell-Bannerman, depressed after his wife's death in August 1906, was himself sick and exhausted. His own instincts stressed the constitutional radicalism of Gladstone, rather than the radicalism of socialism and the Labour party, to which he was at times actively hostile; but he exercised little authority over his cabinet, whose members – most notoriously Grey at the Foreign Office – tended to go their own way. Nevertheless, during the parliamentary sessions of 1906 and 1907 the government forced the Commons to sit up night after night, as it promoted its programme of social reforms, including an Education Bill designed to claw back local authority control over public money spent by Anglican and Roman

Catholic Schools, and the bill to protect Trade Unions from liability for damages resulting from strikes. South Africa was to be given a fully responsible government of its own. Along the way, however, the Liberals became unstuck: in part, because of the last ditch resistance of the Conservatives in the Lords, who took apart the Education Bill and wrecked many of the Liberals' proposals in 1907; in part, by the Irish nationalists' disappointment with the government's proposals for devolution; in part, by the pressure from Labour and the left wing of the Liberal party for further measures of employment reform.

Two heart attacks in 1907 and early 1908 left Campbell-Bannerman unable to cope: Asquith was effectively in charge of the party well before Campbell-Bannerman's resignation in April 1908. Three weeks after it, the former Premier was dead. 'Essentially a *bon vivant, a boulevardier* and a humorist', Margot Asquith called him; but Campbell-Bannerman had grown into his role as the amiable healer of the Liberal party's divisions – even if he had had a part in creating them in the first place.

Herbert Asquith
1852 – 1928

Herbert Henry Asquith was born in 1852, the son of a Yorkshire woollen manufacturer and nonconformist; his father died when he was eight, and Asquith was brought up by his mother and her father. Obviously clever, he was educated at the City of London School, and took a scholarship to Balliol College, Oxford; there in 1874 he was elected to a prize fellowship. In 1877 he married a childhood friend, Helen Melland.

Asquith was set on a political career; the law – he was called to the bar in 1876 – was intended as a stepping-stone towards one. In 1886 he secured, as a Gladstonian Liberal and Home Ruler, a seat at East Fife. Associating with a group of Liberals with imperial leanings and an interest in social reform, among them Edward Grey and R.B. Haldane, Asquith became particularly concerned with Irish questions. In 1888 he appeared as junior counsel for Charles Stewart

Parnell before the Parnell commission investigating the allegations that Parnell had condoned the Phoenix Park murders of 1883. His wife's death in 1891 paved the way to a more ambitious marriage, to Margot Tennant, the vivacious daughter of a Scottish baronet and something of a doyenne of the Liberal party.

Asquith became Home Secretary in Gladstone's 1892 government; but when it was expelled from office, he returned to practice at the Bar. As the Liberal party degenerated into personal squabbles, and successive leaders – Rosebery and Harcourt – resigned, Asquith, though a prominent candidate for the leadership, turned it down. With the Boer War came new divisions within the party: Asquith, with Grey, Haldane and Rosebery, took the imperialist line, demanding from Campbell-Bannerman, the current leader, a more active support for the Salisbury government in its prosecution of the war. But where Rosebery took his opposition to the leadership to the point of secession, Asquith pulled back from that brink: the end of the war, and the reuniting of the party over Balfour's 1902 Education Bill and Joseph Chamberlain's proposals for tariff reform went some way towards healing the rift.

After the fall of the Balfour government in 1905, Asquith accepted the Chancellorship from Campbell-Bannerman, abandoning the attempt of the Liberal imperialists (the 'Limps') to force the Prime Minister into the Lords and out of the limelight. Asquith's budgets of 1906–8 were to begin the process of fiscal reorganisation carried much further by his successor, Lloyd George. In 1906 he began the move towards a graduated income tax; and in 1908 were made the first moves to establish an old age pension. Already acting head of the government during Campbell-Bannerman's frequent absences, Asquith succeeded effortlessly to the leadership when Campbell-Bannerman's illness provoked his resignation in April 1908.

As he arrived in office, the Liberal programme had begun to run into the sand: a failure to pacify the Irish nationalists; government divisions over how much further to carry social reform, and the effective resistance of the Conservative majority in the Lords (which had rejected the Liberal Education Bill in 1906) left the cabinet at a stand. New momentum was found by extending fiscal reform: the Chancellor, Lloyd George's, budget of 1909 was aimed at the traditional Liberal targets, the landlords and the brewers, to raise money for pensions and an expensive plan of naval rearmament. The Lords' shock rejection of the Finance Bill converted the party struggle into a major constitutional crisis. Asquith appealed to the country in a General Election in January 1910. His victory was less convincing than he had hoped: in its wake, the Lords did finally pass the Finance Bill, but Asquith's introduction of the Parliament Bill, designed to restrict the Lords' veto, raised the stakes in the contest. Armed with a promise from the new King, George V, to create more peers in order to secure the passage of the Bill if the government were to win another election on the issue, Asquith dissolved Parliament for the second time in the year. He won the Election – though again by a disappointing margin; revealing the King's undertaking he forced the Bill – barely – through the Lords.

With the drama of the struggle over, Asquith was thrown back onto old Liberal preoccupations. His cautious Irish Home Rule Bill of April 1912, devolving local issues to an Irish assembly, met bitter resistance in Ulster, taking Ireland to the brink of civil war. The outbreak of European war in 1914 left the question shelved. The industrial strikes of 1911-14 showed the government unable to deal with the now sophisticated labour movement; while attempts to return to franchise reform were stymied by its inability to accept women's suffrage. The implication of Lloyd George in the Marconi scandal helped to create the impression of a degenerate government.

But the government's main focus was on foreign affairs. As in much else, here, too, Liberals were divided: between those who urged a pro-French and those who demanded a pro-German stance, and between those who were willing to contemplate British participation in the coming European war, and the pacifists – among them Lloyd George. Britain finally slipped into war after the Bosnian crisis of June 1914; 'we are', Asquith wrote, 'on the eve of horrible things'. Failure to gain a quick victory turned the patriotic mood of the summer sour; Asquith's unassertive style and ineffective war council seemed unable to exercise a proper control over strategy. Allegations of a munitions shortage on the western front and the debacle of the Dardanelles campaign sapped Asquith's political support. To strengthen the government, the Prime Minister in May

1915 constructed a coalition, bringing in Conservatives, and entrusting responsibility for munitions to Lloyd George, who, although he had earlier opposed the war altogether, was now at the head of the demand for all-out war, the 'knock-out blow'.

Arguments over strategy, over conscription (which appalled many Liberals) and over Ireland, in the wake of the Easter Rebellion of 1916, marked the uneasy relationship between the parties in the coalition. Added to these difficulties was disenchantment with Asquith himself. His calmness, so long a virtue, now appeared to be inertia; he had become a heavy drinker (Winston Churchill described him resentfully as 'sodden, supine and supreme'); the death of his son Raymond at the front was a terrible blow to him. In complex intrigues in November and December 1916 Lloyd George, with the wary cooperation of the Conservatives, tried to sideline Asquith, but ultimately made him resign. Most Liberal ministers left with him, leaving Asquith as the leader of the opposition against Lloyd George's essentially Conservative government.

The split among the Liberals was deepened in a debate in May 1918 over the state of the army in France; Asquith's demand for a select committee inquiry was treated by Lloyd George as a matter of confidence. In the post-war election Lloyd George stigmatised those who had voted against the government on the matter as unpatriotic. Asquith's Liberals were wiped out; Asquith himself lost his East Fife seat, and did not return to the Commons until 1920.

The fall of Lloyd George's coalition in 1922 and the Conservative victory at the Election of November 1922, followed by Baldwin's decision to revive the issue of protection, restored Liberal unity, although the party was left after Baldwin's snap election of 1923 as the smallest in Parliament. Asquith lent its support to the eight-month Labour minority government, although Labour rejected a formal coalition and many Liberals were profoundly uncomfortable with the arrangement. The Election which followed the defeat of the MacDonald government in 1924 saw the Liberals cut to a mere forty seats. Asquith was again out of the Commons. Now aged 72, he took a peerage, and entered the House of Lords as Earl of Oxford and Asquith ('Like a suburban villa calling itself Versailles', complained Lady Salisbury). For eighteen months more he remained leader of the Liberal party, squabbling with Lloyd George, most strongly over the line to be taken with the strikers in 1926. In October of that year he resigned the leadership.

The pressure of office had turned Asquith into a drinker whose appearances at the dispatch box could be embarrassing, and had taken him into enthusiastic, almost idolatrous friendships with a number of young women – particularly Venetia Stanley – which verged on the indiscreet. The feud with Lloyd George after 1916 turned a creative political partnership into a highly destructive one, and played a large part in the decline of the Liberal party; yet Asquith's admirers could point to his tactical brilliance and his pre war success in promoting an unprecedented programme of social reforms. Asquith died in February 1928.

David Lloyd George
1863 – 1945

David Lloyd George was born in Manchester in 1863, the son of a schoolmaster, William George. After his father's early death he was brought up in Caernarvonshire by his maternal uncle, a dissenter and radical. He was educated at the local church school, and became a solicitor, well-known locally for his involvement with the chapel, the temperance movement and the Liberal party. In 1888 he married Margaret Owen. Two years later he was returned to parliament for Caernarvon Boroughs.

Campaigning for Welsh self-government, and for the disestablishment of the Anglican Church in Wales, Lloyd George made a name for himself as a fiery, populist radical; but what established his reputation beyond Wales was his vigorous opposition to the Boer War. Lloyd George became the leading 'pro-Boer', in a party deeply divided on the issue, the spokesman of its radical conscience. In Campbell-Bannerman's Liberal ministry of December 1905 he was appointed President of the Board of Trade; three years later Asquith made him Chancellor of the Exchequer. His 'People's Budget' of 1909 blazoned the new Chancellor as the champion of social reform: the shift to a graduated income tax, and taxation on land – and the radical threat which seemed implicit in a promised comprehensive valuation of agricultural land – provoked the large Conservative majority in the House of Lords into rejecting his Finance Bill, and into the confrontation with the Commons which followed, ending in the Parliament Act of 1911. After the defeat of the Peers, Lloyd George continued to press for reform, and in his National Insurance Bill of 1911 offered a contributory health and unemployment insurance scheme. In spite of his political shrewdness and oratorical brilliance, Lloyd George's personal ambition and lack of caution already indicated the threat he posed to the wider interests of his party. At the height of the crisis over the Finance Bill he had conducted his own negotiations with the Conservatives over a coalition; and, never very far away from scandal, he nearly came to grief over his speculation in the shares of Marconi, a government contractor.

Domestic politics were overshadowed by the worsening international situation. Though he was labelled a pacifist because of his stance over the Boer War, and pro-German after the debates of the early 1900s on foreign policy, once he was convinced that war with Germany could not be avoided, Lloyd George threw himself into it. On the formation of the first coalition government in May 1915, Lloyd George was made Minister of Munitions, throwing his energy into the enormous task of supplying the troops; in July 1916 he moved to be Secretary of State for War, just at the beginning of the battle of the Somme. His concern at British strategy and Asquith's conduct of the war mounted. He had already been brought closer to the Conservatives within the coalition through his support for conscription, which had been strenuously resisted by most of the Liberals; in December 1916, he collaborated with them to depose the Prime Minister, although the effect had been not entirely intended. Lloyd George replaced him; most of the Liberals in the cabinet resigned with their leader, and Lloyd George was left at the head of a government of the

Conservatives, Labour, and the rump of the Liberals.

He came into office at almost the worst moment in the war, with stalemate on the Western Front, and heavy losses at sea; his own party having deserted him, his authority within his own government was weak. He replaced the cabinet of twenty-three with a small war cabinet of five, which he was able to dominate, and he formed a close relationship with Bonar Law, the Conservative leader. The entry of the United States into the War in 1917 almost guaranteed eventual success; but in the meantime, the bloody and indecisive battles of Ypres and Passchendaele had to be endured. The Prime Minister's poor relationship with the British commander-in-chief, Haig, led him to press for a unified allied command: the great German offensive in mid-1918 all but forced one on the allies anyway. When peace came, rather unexpectedly in November, it appeared a personal triumph for Lloyd George.

Before the war was won, Lloyd George had already had an eye to the political future. Without a political base of his own (now that Asquith had taken with him the bulk of the Liberals), he prepared for a post-war General Election by cementing his alliance with Bonar Law. Although it signalled Lloyd George's personal popularity, the 'coupon election' (in which the two government leaders helped to ensure the election of chosen candidates by giving them certificates of their loyalty to the wartime coalition) embittered the Liberal schism while still leaving him weak. It was the Conservatives who in practice benefited.

Lloyd George remained Prime Minister, dominating the government (to the irritation of his colleagues), and dominating the negotiations which led to the Treaty of Versailles. At home, the brief boom of post-war reconstruction was succeeded, by 1921, by a nasty slump. In the aftermath of the Irish Rebellion of 1916, the victory of the separatist Republican party, Sinn Fein, at the 1918 Election made a solution of the Irish situation more urgent than ever. The guerrilla warfare between British forces and the IRA which followed Sinn Fein's declaration of independence was brutal even by the standards of previous Irish history; only in 1921 did a compromise emerge, at the last possible moment.

Lloyd George's hold over what was in effect a Conservative government was throughout these years increasingly shaky. Bonar Law's resignation in 1921 for health reasons removed its mainstay. The cabinet became divided over relations with Soviet Russia, and the Prime Minister was dogged by the scandal over his granting of honours in return for contributions to his party's funds. The restiveness of Conservative backbenchers came to a head in 1922 as Lloyd George appeared ready to go to war against Turkey to defend the settlement of the Near East of the Treaty of Sèvres. The famous meeting at the Carlton Club in October resulted in their decision to repudiate the coalition. Lloyd George resigned the same day.

The election which ensued left Lloyd George and Asquith leading Liberal factions roughly equal in number. Baldwin's revival of the issue of protection brought about an uneasy reconciliation. The factions stood together for the 1923 election, but relations between Asquith and Lloyd George never really recovered. The two finally split over Asquith's condemnation of the General Strike of 1926, and Asquith resigned the leadership, leaving Lloyd George in full possession, energetically planning the party's revival with a campaign against unemployment. But Liberal support and seats declined again in the 1929 Election; rather than go through another, the party helped to prop up Ramsay MacDonald's administration. Illness prevented Lloyd George from participating in the formation of the National Government in 1931. Deprecating the decision of the Liberals who did join it to agree to a dissolution that year, he watched as the party divided over Tariff Reform and was slaughtered at the polls. Afterwards, he resigned the leadership.

Lloyd George remained vigorous in retirement, writing, promoting solutions to unemployment, opposing rearmament, and becoming an enthusiastic admirer of Hitler - 'a magnetic, dynamic personality with a single purpose' - and the economic success of his Germany. After his wife's death, he married his long-standing secretary and mistress, Frances Stevenson. In 1945 he finally left the House of Commons, accepting a peerage as Earl Lloyd George of Dwyfor. Not long afterwards he died. Few Prime Ministers have aroused quite such strong reactions as Lloyd George: his magnetic and forceful personality, coupled with an enormous appetite for power, helped both to carry Britain through the First World War, and to destroy the Liberal party.

Andrew Bonar Law
1858 – 1923

Andrew Bonar Law was born in 1858 in Canada, the son of a Presbyterian minister from Ulster; not until he was twelve did he come to Britain, with his aunt (his mother had died when he was two). He was educated at Glasgow High School; at sixteen he entered a family firm of merchant bankers, and settled down to a career in business. In 1891 he married Annie Pitcairn Robley. In 1898 he was elected as the Unionist candidate for the Blackfriars and Hutchesontown division of Glasgow. He soon found office – Parliamentary Secretary to the Board of Trade – and a cause – Joseph Chamberlain's scheme for colonial preference and tariff reform. When Chamberlain was incapacitated by a stroke in 1907, he succeeded to Chamberlain's mantle as the most ardent proponent of tariff reform; at the same time, he became one of the strongest defenders of the Ulster Protestants against the Liberals' Irish Home Rule proposals.

On Balfour's resignation as Conservative leader in November 1911, Bonar Law was elected the leader of the parliamentary party, a compromise candidate between its old Tory and progressive wings. Bonar Law cut an odd figure among the Tory grandees, and had little standing in the party beyond a reputation as a vigorous debater. A fellow Canadian, the millionaire businessman Max Aitken (later Lord Beaverbrook) had helped to gain him the leadership and to smooth his path within it.

Law's tough opposition to the Liberals, particularly on Irish Home Rule, was in striking contrast to Balfour's rather ethereal musings, and won him the praise of his party. But Law's expressions of sympathy with the Ulstermen's preparations to resist home rule came dangerously close to incitement to rebellion; Law was attempting to step back from this position as the situation in Ireland became more and more dangerous when, opportunely, if not fortunately, the outbreak of the first World War swept the issue aside. Law committed his party to loyal support for the Liberal government of Asquith during the war; by 1915, however, as the Unionist backbenchers became restive, the need for the government to have a firmer base of support in Parliament became plain. Asquith formed a coalition, although the Liberals retained the principal offices, and Law had to be satisfied with the Secretaryship for the colonies. An uneasy alliance developed between him and Lloyd George as criticism grew of Asquith's style and conduct of the war. In the confused ministerial crisis of December 1916, the two provoked Asquith's resignation (and those of most of the Liberal ministers). Lloyd George became premier, and Bonar Law became his Chancellor of the Exchequer and Leader of the Commons.

Cooperation turned the partnership of two outsiders into a warm friendship. Lloyd George was effectively maintained in power by Unionist consent alone, and he succeeded in obtaining the agreement of Bonar Law that the Liberal and Conservative members of the coalition should fight the election of 1918 in partnership. They won it with a majority of nearly 250. Lloyd George continued as Prime Minister, and Bonar Law became Lord Privy Seal, continuing as Leader of the Commons, and deputising for the Prime Minister during his frequent absences abroad. Despite the resentment of the right wing of the Conservative party at working under Lloyd George, the coalition survived over the immediate post-war period. But Law's resignation in 1921 because of ill-health, and his replacement by the lofty Austen Chamberlain triggered its disintegration. When Lloyd George seemed about to go to war with Turkey in 1922 the Conservative backbenchers finally revolted. Law, concerned above all else to preserve the party's unity, reluctantly, but decisively, backed their condemnation of the coalition at the famous October meeting at the Carlton Club. Lloyd George resigned, and (once he had been elected into the party leadership) Bonar Law succeeded him as Prime Minister at the head of a purely Conservative government. He immediately called a General Election. Campaigning on a slogan of 'tranquillity', the Conservatives won a convincing majority.

Law's low-key premiership was as different as it was possible to be from Lloyd George's flamboyance. It came into existence just as negotiations between Britain and France over Germany's default on its war reparations broke down. In January 1923 France occupied the Ruhr, and Anglo-French relations fell to rock-bottom. At the same time, America was pressing for repayment of the British war debt: reluctantly, and under protest, Law acceded to the views of the rest of the cabinet and the City that Britain should accept the harsh repayment terms offered by the United States. Law's illness – a cancer of the throat – reasserted itself, and in May 1923 he resigned, ending a premiership that had lasted a mere 209 days. By the end of October he was dead.

Stanley Baldwin
1867 – 1947

Stanley Baldwin was born in 1867, the son of Alfred Baldwin, a Worcestershire ironmaster and member of Parliament, and his wife Louisa MacDonald – one of a talented and artistic family which connected Baldwin to Rudyard Kipling and Sir Edward Burne-Jones. Baldwin was educated at Harrow and Trinity College, Cambridge. In 1892 he married Lucy, daughter of Edward Ridsdale. His poor degree left him little alternative to entry into the family business; but involvement in the business took him into local politics. On the death of his father in 1908, he succeeded, without a contest, to his father's old constituency, the Bewdley division of Worcestershire.

Baldwin earned some respect, but made little impact, in the Commons. His appointment in 1916 as Parliamentary Private Secretary to Bonar Law (then Chancellor in the coalition headed by Lloyd George) was owing to his discretion and availability, rather than any more brilliant political qualities: but his efficiency brought him in 1917 the job of deputising for Sir Hardman Lever, the Financial Secretary to the Treasury. On Law's retirement in 1921 Law urged Lloyd George to take him in to the cabinet, and Lloyd George obliged, making him President of the Board of Trade. The year which followed was a formative one for Baldwin. His revulsion for the style and leadership of Lloyd George became intense; at the famous Carlton Club meeting of October 1922, Baldwin was the only cabinet minister to support the backbench revolt against the government which effectively destroyed the coalition, and split the Conservatives into pro- and anti-coalition wings. 'A dynamic force', he said of Lloyd George, 'is a very terrible thing; it may crush you but it is not necessarily right'.

Baldwin thus made his reputation within the party; Bonar Law made him Chancellor in the government which replaced the coalition, and he played a large part in the Conservative Election victory of November. Despite Baldwin's inexperience, and Law's dislike for the unfavourable terms which Baldwin accepted for the repayment of the American war debt, the Chancellor acted as deputy for the Prime Minister as his illness took hold of him. When Law gave up in May 1923, the claims of Lord Curzon, the Foreign Secretary, to succeed him were overlooked, and Baldwin accepted the premiership – self-deprecatingly, but imbued with an almost religious determination to cast out the corruption which he saw pervading British politics.

Baldwin's decision to call a general election a few months after his accession appeared quixotic and out of character in so cautious and unflamboyant a politician. In part it reflected his conviction that unemployment could only be combated by the imposition of protective tariffs – a policy which Law had in 1922 ruled out without a specific mandate. In part it simply reflected his desire to win a popular affirmation of the change of leader. He was sorely disappointed. The result of the December 1923 election was the loss of the government's overall majority. Less concerned than his colleagues at the prospect of a first Labour government, Baldwin rejected schemes to keep them out of power, handing over to MacDonald in January 1924.

Despite resentment in his own party, the absence of an acceptable alternative helped Baldwin to retain its leadership. In the Election of 1924, helped by the discrediting of the Labour party with the fake 'Zinoviev letter', it was returned to office with a commanding majority.

Baldwin's first task was to reunite his party, and he brought into the government not only the losers of the argument in 1922, but also Winston Churchill, who had departed from the Conservatives in 1904. More broadly, Baldwin declared his commitment to 'the binding together of all classes of our people in an effort to make life in this country better in every sense of the word. That is the main end and object of my life in politics'. But growing industrial unrest, particularly among the miners, made it a difficult promise to keep. In 1925 the cabinet bought off the miners; but in 1926, negotiations between the miners, the TUC and the government broke down. Baldwin was well-prepared for confrontation with a half-hearted TUC, and the General Strike was over in little more than a week. His victory against the Strike brought him considerable prestige, though it was tarnished by the fact that the miners' dispute dragged on for six more months, and by a Trades Disputes Act which was interpreted as a vindictive exploitation of the government's victory. As the Parliament rolled on, with an enormous majority protecting the government from all but its own supporters, Baldwin was accused of torpidity and lack of leadership, despite his personal popularity. At the General Election of May 1929 the government was defeated, its slogan 'safety first' rousing no-one.

Defeat revived the animus of his enemies within the Conservative party. Imperialists fought determinedly against his acceptance of Labour's policy of granting India dominion status; the press barons, Lords Beaverbrook and Rothermere, waged a feud against him partly focussed on an imperial tariff preference scheme. But Baldwin clung on, facing down the revolts. In August 1931 the Labour government finally collapsed, unable to agree on a response to the financial crisis which was forcing Britain off the gold standard. Baldwin, with the Liberal leader, Sir Herbert Samuel (Lloyd George was ill), agreed to join MacDonald in forming a national government to take the unpopular measures necessary to deal with the crisis. Baldwin took office as Lord President of the

Council. In the election of October, the coalition (or mainly the Conservative element within it) won a landslide victory.

Free from significant departmental duties, Baldwin, though the real power in the government, could concentrate on what interested him most. The enactment of a protectionist – or imperial preference – scheme was largely the work of his understudy and rival, Neville Chamberlain; but the coaxing of Conservatives to support the granting of dominion status to India in 1935 was his own achievement. MacDonald, visibly in decline, passed the premiership on to him in 1935. Timing an election to coincide with the celebrations of George V's silver jubilee, he won another large majority.

By 1935, the menacing aspect of European politics made the refurbishment of British defences urgent. Baldwin recognised that as much as most, although his fine nose for public opinion made him approach the subject cautiously. At the Election, and after it, Baldwin edged the country away from confidence in the conflict-solving efficacy of the League of Nations and towards a modest programme of rearmament. His commitment to resist the aggression of the continental dictatorships was a little undermined by the revelation shortly after the election of a deal made by the Foreign Secretary, Sir Samuel Hoare, effectively to abandon most of Abyssinia to Mussolini. A far-reaching programme of rearmament was published in March 1936, just as Hitler's troops reoccupied the Rhineland, demilitarised under the 1919 Treaty of Versailles. At about the same time, a domestic crisis called for all Baldwin's renowned tact and sensitivity. He tried hard to overcome the determination of the new King, Edward VIII, to marry the twice-divorced Mrs Simpson, but when he failed, he firmly refused to countenance any of the schemes which were devised in order to allow him to marry and to remain King.

Baldwin was seventy, and ready to retire. He stayed on to see in the new King, George VI, and resigned on the fourteenth anniversary of his election as leader of the Conservative party, in May 1937, and received an earldom, as Earl Baldwin of Bewdley. He died in 1947.

When war came, much of the odium for the forces' unpreparedness was heaped on Baldwin – unfairly, for he had, as much as most others, sought in the mid–to–late thirties to revive British defence capacity. Yet his decency and patent goodwill seemed to many unsuited for the job of running a major industrial power, his homespun philosophy and cosy images of rural England inappropriate for a country attempting to climb back to economic recovery. Politicians, he once remarked, 'rather resemble Alice in Wonderland, who tried to play croquet with a flamingo instead of a mallet'. Baldwin's politics, felt his many critics, were likely to achieve as much as Alice's croquet.

James Ramsay MacDonald
1866 – 1937

James Ramsay MacDonald was born in October 1866, the illegitimate son of a farmgirl, Anne Ramsay, and John MacDonald, a highlander from Ross. Despite his inauspicious origin, MacDonald's determination and Lossiemouth education took him, through a series of clerical jobs into occasional journalism and political involvement – in the Marxist Social Democratic Federation, the Fabian society, and Keir Hardie's new Independent Labour Party. Marriage in 1896 to Margaret Gladstone, the daughter of the distinguished scientist John Hall Gladstone, brought him financial security and time for politics, as well as the influence and support of an intelligent, sociable and socialist wife. MacDonald was elected in 1900 as Secretary of the Labour Representation Committee, the alliance between the Trades Union Congress, the Independent Labour Party, the Social Democratic Federation and the Fabian Society which was intended to secure the representation of the labour movement in Parliament. In 1903, he won from the Liberals a commitment to offer no opposition to the Committee's candidates in about thirty seats: as a result, at the 1906 election, twenty-five of its supporters (including MacDonald himself) were returned, now known as the Labour party, but nevertheless supporting the Liberal government. In 1911 he became Chairman of the parliamentary labour group, struggling manfully to keep the Labour-Liberal pact on the rails. But he also, devastatingly, lost his wife.

MacDonald's condemnation of British involvement in the First World War resulted in his resignation from the Chairmanship when the party came out in favour of it in August 1914; branded a pacifist, MacDonald argued for a negotiated peace. For a time the party split into pro- and anti-war factions. Although the schism had been largely repaired by 1918, in the election of that year, MacDonald's wartime stance lost him his seat. Despite his defeat, MacDonald became more influential in the labour movement outside Parliament, helping to prevent the Independent Labour Party joining the Communist International. He returned to the Commons at the General Election of 1922, taking a seat at Aberavon. His reputation as an effective debater and parliamentary tactician won him the Chairmanship of the Parliamentary Labour Party, and in effect, the leadership of the official opposition.

Baldwin's miscalculated General Election of 1923 gave MacDonald the chance to be something more. The Conservatives were left without an overall majority, and Labour was the second largest party. Both Asquith and Baldwin ignored the complex machinations inside the Conservative and Liberal parties which were designed to keep Labour out of power. MacDonald rejected a formal agreement with the Liberals, although for their own purposes both they and the Conservatives contrived for the moment to permit Labour to govern. Anxious to be seen as moderate and unrevolutionary, MacDonald eschewed a radical programme of socialist reform, concentrating his own energies abroad. Retaining to himself the office of Foreign Secretary, he presided over the settlement of German reparations in September 1924. The Conservatives and Liberals finally foreclosed on the first Labour government in September 1924, bringing about its defeat on a motion concerning the failure to prosecute a Communist journalist under the Incitement to Mutiny Act. MacDonald welcomed the chance of a new General Election, which might clarify the confused party situation, and would prevent an inevitable split between his own right and left wings. The Conservative victory was predictable (the publication of a forged letter, supposedly from the Bolshevik Zinoviev to the Labour government, made little difference to the result); but the Election of 1924, while losing Labour forty seats, achieved MacDonald's objective in destroying the Liberals' prospects of forming a government.

Despite the resentment of left-wingers at the party's failure when in government to promote a programme of reform, MacDonald easily confirmed his hold over the party and had his view of its aims and identity endorsed by it. Though he was apprehensive about the effect on Labour's electoral support of the 1926 General Strike, the inactivity of Baldwin's government in the face of severe unemployment helped the party to come within twenty-one votes of achieving an overall majority in the General Election of 1928, and Macdonald formed a government, although he was again locked into an inconvenient alliance of convenience with the Liberals. MacDonald continued to be personally preoccupied with foreign affairs, although he did not (as he had done in 1924) himself hold the Foreign Secretaryship, but gave it instead to Arthur Henderson, one of the party's principal strategists. Early in his Premiership MacDonald visited the United States, establishing a rapport with President Hoover. At home the government proceeded only in a stately fashion to tackle long-term unemployment: its efforts were rapidly overtaken by events, as the Wall Street Crash of October 1929 initiated a major world-wide slump, sending unemployment rocketing and the government's popularity plunging. Its response was confused. Sir Oswald Moseley, a junior minister with partial responsibility for employment policy, resigned over its failure to adopt his programme including an extension of state control over industry, protection and programmes of public works. In the summer of 1931, the collapse of an Austrian bank caused a further international financial crisis: funds flowed out of London. The government could choose either to abandon the fixed exchange rate of the Gold Standard and devalue the currency, or to seek the support of foreign banks to help support the pound. To attract foreign capital, the government committed itself to a series of deep cuts in public expenditure. With determined opposition both from the cabinet and the TUC, MacDonald felt unable to continue as the government was presently constituted. Offering his resignation to the King, he accepted his commission to form a new government with the support of Liberals and Conservatives. The party instantly split: a few ministers remained loyal; the majority of the cabinet and the rest of the party repudiated MacDonald as a traitor, and appointed Henderson as leader.

MacDonald formed a cabinet with four Conservatives, two Liberals and three other Labour ministers. Ironically, it was soon forced to abandon the Gold Standard anyway. Nevertheless, the 'National' government caught a sombre mood in the country: in the General Election of October 1931 it won by a landslide, smashing the Labour party's strength. The vast majority of its seats were Conservative ones, and although MacDonald was unhappy to find himself, in effect, a captive of the Conservatives, his personal popularity remained important for the government. But its 'national' character soon decayed. The free-trade supporting Liberals left after a series of preferential tariff agreements were reached at Ottawa in the summer of 1932. MacDonald had even more reason than before to confine himself largely to foreign affairs, and he was deeply involved in the process which led to the granting of provincial self-government to India in the India Bill of 1935, and in the disarmament summitry which Hitler's rise to power in Germany rendered pointless.

From 1933, MacDonald began to grow ill – 'dwindling into senility' wrote Churchill. In 1935 he stepped down as Prime Minister. With little else but politics to live for, MacDonald pathetically clung on to office, as Lord President, until 1937. He died a few months after his resignation. MacDonald's triumphant leadership of the Labour party into its first two periods of office had ended in acrimony and failure: his rather vague socialism and his anxiety not to jeopardise Labour's electoral chances by seriously rocking the boat had prevented the party from espousing any clear policy in response to the grim economic climate of the late 1920s; his coalition of 1931 was seen by his colleagues as a basic betrayal of its principal aims. But the Labour party owed much to MacDonald, whose dedication and caution had helped to convert it into a serious political force.

Neville Chamberlain
1869 – 1940

Neville Chamberlain was born in 1869, the son of Joseph Chamberlain, the campaigner for Tariff Reform who had split the Conservative party in 1903, and his second wife. Austen, Neville's elder half-brother, had been marked by their father for the high office which he himself had never attained: Neville was educated at Rugby and Mason College (later to be Birmingham University) and packed off to plant a sisal crop on his father's estate in the Bahamas. The project was a failure, and he returned to Birmingham in 1897. Chamberlain settled down into a career in manufacturing and got married, in 1911, to Annie Cole; but he also became closely concerned with Birmingham municipal politics. In 1911 he was elected to the City council, and in 1915 became Mayor. A reputation as an active and efficient administrator caught the attention of the national government, and Lloyd George appointed him to organise a scheme of voluntary labour for war industries. The appointment was not a success: Chamberlain and Lloyd George, diametrically opposed personalities, failed to understand one another, and Chamberlain resigned within seven months. Lloyd George complained that Chamberlain was 'a man of rigid competency... lost in an emergency or creative tasks at any time'; Chamberlain formed a deep distrust of Lloyd George.

Chamberlain progressed from local to national politics in the General Election of December 1918, when he was returned to the House of Commons for the Ladywood division in Birmingham, as a Conservative. After the fall of the coalition government and Lloyd George, in October 1922, Chamberlain was brought into Bonar Law's ministry, partly as an olive branch to his brother Austen, the loser in the party's Carlton Club rebellion against the coalition. He climbed fast: he was appointed Postmaster-General, then Paymaster-General, then Minister of Health. Discovering both an aptitude for and an attachment to the latter job, he was unwillingly dragged out of it to become in 1923 Chancellor of the Exchequer; but after the short period of Labour government in 1924 he could insist to Baldwin that he should return to Health. His inside-out knowledge of the complexities of local government and the social-reforming impulses which he had inherited from his father made him ideal for the job. Over the next five years he carried through an extension of the national insurance system and a thorough reform of the poor law and local government. His department was at the centre of the government's domestic policy, and he effectively became the dominant figure. Loyal to Baldwin, he was nevertheless dubious about the Prime Minister's qualities of leadership, and impatient with his irresolution during the General Strike and his failure to build on its defeat.

By 1929, Chamberlain was generally regarded as Baldwin's natural successor. After the Conservative defeat in the General Election of that year (Chamberlain abandoned the working-class Ladywood seat for the more genteel Edgbaston) he was appointed party Chairman and continued with the programme of organisational reforms instituted by his predecessor. But the Labour schism of 1931 brought Conservatives back into government in the MacDonald coalition, and helped to ensure them a massive election success. Chamberlain became

Chancellor once more, able finally to satisfy, at least in part, his father's call for tariff reform and a system of imperial preference, and, after a few years of strict economy, presiding over a modest recovery from the vicious world slump. As Chancellor, Chamberlain had been closely involved in the debates within the government over rearmament, and was responsible for wielding the Treasury axe against the proposals of a 1934 defence review. Chamberlain's conviction of the economic and political impossibility of creating the capability to fight all three major threats – Germany, Italy and Japan – formed the background to his pursuit of negotiations with the continental dictators after he finally succeeded to the premiership on Baldwin's resignation in 1937.

Chamberlain's assessment of the international situation was a conventional one: the advocates of a more confrontational approach to Hitler or Mussolini or the Japanese (such as Winston Churchill) were still generally marginal figures. Chamberlain shared the revulsion at the despotisms governing Germany and Italy; but his anxiety to avoid a repetition of the last terrible war, and his conviction that the causes of European friction lay essentially in justifiable grievances between rational people led him to travel further down the path of appeasement than many of his contemporaries believed was either honourable or sensible.

Such differences in perception were only in part responsible for the resignation of the Foreign Secretary, Sir Anthony Eden, in February 1938. Eden was also piqued by the Prime Minister's refusal to leave him and foreign policy alone. A European conflagration appeared to become truly imminent in March 1938, with the Anschluss, Hitler's annexation of Austria. There were clear indications that Hitler's next target would be Czechoslovakia, supposedly in defence of the majority ethnic German population of its Sudetenland. Czechoslovakia was hedged about by international guarantees from France and Russia, and France and Britain made clear their objections to any use of force – clear enough for it to seem in the summer that European war was about to break out. Yet Chamberlain felt strongly against British action in Czechoslovakia, even if military advice had been more favourable towards it. It was, he said famously, 'a quarrel in a far-away country between people of whom we know nothing'. Throughout September Chamberlain engaged in a dramatic shuttle diplomacy with Hitler and France which culminated at Munich on the 30th with the Czechs' reluctant agreement to cede the Sudetenland balanced by international guarantees of the remainder of their state. Chamberlain also came back with Hitler's signature on the notorious 'piece of paper' declaring that Britain and Germany were resolved never again to go to war.

Chamberlain's agreement, which he described as 'peace with honour... peace for our time', was acclaimed by the press, but sparked a bitter debate in political circles. It lasted less than six months. In March 1939 Hitler invaded Czechoslovakia, and even Chamberlain began to recognise the need for a firm stance. As Hitler seemed to be ready to move against Poland, Britain and France concluded a provisional agreement to lend Poland assistance if she were attacked. Chamberlain reluctantly approached the Soviet Union to secure its support, but was beaten to it by the Nazi-Soviet pact of August. On 1 September 1939 Hitler invaded Poland; two days later Chamberlain declared war.

It became clear that the Prime Minister was not the man to fight the war. For one thing, its outbreak represented the failure of the policy with which he had been so closely identified; for another, it was to require a cooperation with the representatives of organised labour which Chamberlain – whose contempt for most of the left was not concealed – was eminently unlikely to obtain. The failure of the Norwegian campaign in April 1940 brought together his critics, both on the opposition and the Conservative benches. When Labour divided the House at the end of the debate of 7/8 May, although Chamberlain won the vote, the number of abstentions and rebellions on the government side made it clear that he could not retain the confidence of his party; and the Labour leaders subsequently made it clear that neither were they prepared to support him. He resigned on 10 May.

Chamberlain survived his resignation only a few months: he died on 9 November. Chamberlain's pursuit of appeasement had come to seem not only misguided, but disgraceful; in 1940 he appeared not just wrong, but also one of the 'guilty men'. Chamberlain's abrasive, confrontational style added to the odium in which he was generally held. Though unusually clear-sighted, he had become rigidly attached to his analysis of the international situation, and unable to alter it when it had become obviously inappropriate.

Sir Winston Churchill
1874 – 1965

Sir Winston Churchill was born in 1874, the son of Lord Randolph Churchill, the burnt-out star of the Conservative party, and his wife, an American, Jennie Jerome. He was educated at Harrow and Sandhurst, then commissioned into the army. Energetic and adventurous, he saw action on the Indian frontier and at Omdurman; and, after resigning his commission in 1899, he worked as a journalist and fought as an irregular in the Boer War.

Already enjoying a reputation as war hero and daredevil, Churchill was elected for Oldham as a Unionist in the General election of 1900. But in the convulsions within the Conservative party over Joseph Chamberlain's tariff reform proposals of 1903, Churchill, with a number of other free-traders, crossed to the Liberals. He adopted with enthusiasm his new party's populist, but paternalist, programme of social reform. Campbell-Bannerman made him

Parliamentary Under-Secretary for the Colonies in 1906; Asquith brought him into the cabinet in 1908, as President of the Board of Trade, where he worked closely with Lloyd George on the unemployment insurance scheme; and in 1910 he was made Home Secretary. In the meantime, Churchill had married Clementine, the daughter of Colonel Sir Henry Hozier, a wife who was to become a formidable political partner.

Churchill swapped jobs with the first Lord of the Admiralty, McKenna, in 1911. He proceeded to reorganise the Navy Board, and (over the heads and dead bodies of many senior officers) to modernise the navy. Churchill was still at the Admiralty when war broke out, and from there he promoted his own project of opening a second front in the Dardanelles. Its failure was his downfall, as the Conservatives (whose rancour stemmed originally from his apostasy) demanded his removal as part of the price for joining a coalition in 1915 – although Churchill remained in the government in a more junior role until he resigned in frustration and went to join the army in Flanders.

He was recalled by Lloyd George in July 1917, to be successively Minister of Munitions, Secretary of State for War, and for the Colonies. The post-war years saw him waging an obsessive, but unsuccessful battle to persuade the cabinet to give its full support to the opponents of the Bolshevik revolution in Russia. In 1922, after Lloyd George's coalition was brought down by the backbench Conservative revolt at the Carlton Club, Churchill found himself without office; in the Election at the end of the year, he found himself without a seat.

A year in the wilderness, the arrival of a minority Labour government in January 1924 ('a serious national misfortune'), and Baldwin's abandonment of Tariff Reform following the 1923 Election defeat, reconciled Churchill to Conservative party. The party was far from entirely reconciled to him, but Baldwin nevertheless made him Chancellor of the Exchequer – to Churchill's own astonishment. Succumbing to economic orthodoxy, Churchill took sterling back to the Gold Standard, but with unhappy results. His attempts at drastic defence cuts were repudiated by Baldwin, as were his attempts at conciliation after the General Strike of 1926 (Churchill – with his usual exuberance – had been in the forefront of the measures to beat the strike). After the Labour victory in the Election of 1929 Churchill's opposition to the granting of dominion status to India, the policy of both Labour and the Conservatives, left him once more out in the cold. In his other campaign, for rearmament and against appeasement of the European dictators, Churchill was practically, until 1938, a lone voice. By 1939 his prescience seemed obvious: he was called back to the Admiralty on the German invasion of Poland, and though he had been out of office for ten years, he established himself irresistibly as the essential war leader.

Churchill's rise to power came as a result of a backbench Conservative rebellion in May 1940 and the refusal of the Labour party to serve in a coalition led by Neville Chamberlain. On 10 May he was appointed Prime Minister at the head of a national government made up of Labour and the Conservatives. The illness and resignation of Chamberlain in October consolidated his hold over the Conservative party; a series of powerful speeches conveyed to the nation by radio or by print, consolidated his hold over the country. Churchill was a prolific and stylish author: in the early 1920s he had written (among other things) a monumental account of the first war; after the Second World War he was to write an enormous history of that, too. His wartime speeches, though, were his rhetorical masterpieces, whether they were inspiring the British in the worst moments of the conflict with his pledge that 'we shall fight on the landing grounds, we shall fight in the fields and in the streets, we shall fight in the hills, we shall never surrender' or encouraging the forces with his tribute that 'never in the field of human conflict was so much owed by so many to so few'.

Churchill threw himself into leadership with characteristic energy, involving himself sometimes usefully, sometimes disastrously, in all government business. But he occupied himself mainly with military strategy: the home front he left largely to the Labour partners in the coalition, particularly Ernest Bevin and Clement Attlee. The early years of the war, 1940 and 1941, saw Britain, in Churchill's phrase, with her back to the wall, barely beating off the Blitz, her Atlantic supply lines only just kept open against mounting losses to submarines. Hitler invaded Russia in June 1941, and Churchill found a new ally despite his hostility to Bolshevism. In December Japanese attacks on British forces and possessions in South-East Asia opened a new front and spelt the beginning of the end of the British Empire; but the attack on Pearl Harbour brought America into the war – and, Churchill believed, saved Britain. Allied strategy was set in a series of summits. In Washington in December 1941 Churchill and Roosevelt worked out the details of Anglo-American collaboration; in January 1943, at Casablanca, they resolved on Churchill's own project, the invasion of Italy, 'the soft underbelly of the axis', which proved rather more muscular than he had thought. In early 1944, however, the American scheme for the invasion of France was given priority; by February 1945, France was liberated and the war in Europe almost over. The second and last meeting of the three allied leaders at Yalta agreed on the occupation of Germany and the establishment of the United Nations.

Germany's defeat brought to an end Churchill's tenure of power. His wartime achievement won him immense stature; but he was unresponsive to the mood of social reform which the war had stimulated and which had inspired the Beveridge Report on Social Welfare in 1942 and the Education Act of 1944. With the war in Europe finished, neither Labour nor Conservatives had much desire to prolong the coalition government. Churchill called an election for July; confident of success, but misjudging the mood of the electorate, he was heavily defeated. He became an Olympian leader of the opposition: he won wide attention for his solemn warnings against the Soviet bloc (his famous 'iron curtain' speech was delivered in America in 1946) and his championing of European unity, but the day-to-day business of opposing the government he left in the hands of others. The Conservatives recovered slowly from their defeat of 1945: in 1950 they eroded Labour's majority to six; and in October 1951 Attlee tried another election. Churchill, at seventy-six, was returned to power with a majority of seventeen.

Relaxing wartime controls, the government enjoyed an economic boom; even had it wished to, though, the thin majority precluded it from attempting to alter Labour's welfare reforms. Churchill continued to concern himself chiefly with foreign affairs. Stalin's death in 1953 seemed to promise an unfreezing of the Cold War, and Churchill hoped to crown his career by ending it. But President Eisenhower vetoed a negotiation and that was that (and a confirmation of how far Britain had already slipped into a deferential, if special, relationship with the

United States). The alternative to the special relationship, closer involvement with Europeans, seemed less attractive than it had been in the 1940s – at least Churchill did nothing to further the proposed European Defence Community in 1952, although the project was ultimately scotched in the French National Assembly.

Churchill was not only an old man, but a sick one. He made a good recovery from a stroke in 1953; but in 1955 he was finally persuaded to retire, handing on the leadership to Eden. He remained in the House of Commons until his death in 1965.

Clement Attlee
1883 – 1967

Clement Attlee was born in Putney in 1883, the son of a city solicitor. He was educated at Haileybury College and University College, Oxford, and was called to the bar in 1905. Much of his spare time he spent working at Haileybury House, a boy's club in the East End of London supported by his old school. The experience helped to make him a socialist, and led him (with the help of an independent income after his father's death) into a number of jobs connected with social work. By 1908 he had joined the Independent Labour Party. During the First World War he served in Gallipoli, Mesopotamia and Northern France, and rose to the rank of Major; at its end, he returned to the East End, becoming mayor of Stepney in 1919.

In 1922 he was married to Violet Millar, and was elected to the House of Commons, for Limehouse. Attlee's profession, and his professionalism, were uncommon at the time in the Parliamentary Labour Party; its leader Ramsay MacDonald made him one of his Parliamentary Private Secretaries, and in the minority Labour Government of 1923-4, he was Under-Secretary for War. Attlee, competent but quiet, was not, however, an obvious candidate for very high office, and after Labour returned to power in 1929 he was not at first given a post at all. It was almost a year before he was made Chancellor of the Duchy of Lancaster. The party's split in March 1931 after MacDonald formed the National Government, and the removal of most of the party's leadership in the disastrous General Election later the same year, left Attlee as one of its few Members of Parliament with ministerial experience. It elected a new leader, George Lansbury, and a deputy, Attlee. Much of the parliamentary burden fell on Attlee and his former ministerial colleague, Stafford Cripps. The pacifist Lansbury resigned the leadership in 1935 after defeat at the party conference over the response to Mussolini's invasion of Abyssinia. Attlee was chosen as his temporary replacement, and despite Labour's disappointing performance in the 1935 General Election, he beat challenges from two ministers who had recovered their seats, Herbert Morrison and Arthur Greenwood, to be confirmed in the leadership.

Cautious and unassertive, Attlee stood back from the fierce arguments over cooperation with the Communists and the Independent Labour Party (which had seceded from the Labour mainstream in 1932) which led to the expulsion of Cripps and Aneurin Bevan in 1939; likewise he acted merely as a moderator between the rearming and disarming wings of the party, represented respectively by Hugh Dalton and Ernest Bevin on the one hand, and Morrison on the other. By 1937 the party and Attlee had come down clearly on the side of rearmament and against appeasement. On the outbreak of war, the Labour National Executive Committee decided not to join Chamberlain's national government, and made no effort to disguise their dislike of the Prime Minister (which was certainly reciprocated). Their reiteration of that refusal after Chamberlain's support on the Conservative back-benches was shown to be ebbing away in May 1940 prompted the Prime Minister's resignation. Churchill took his place, and invited Labour into a coalition.

Attlee served successively as Lord Privy Seal, Secretary of State for the

Dominions, and Lord President of the Council. As Churchill's deputy he chaired the cabinet in the Prime Minister's frequent absences abroad; while Churchill attended to military strategy, Attlee presided over the home front. Wartime mobilisation went some way to achieving Labour goals of full employment and state management of the economy, and as victory came in sight, Labour ministers began to plan ways of consolidating these changes and furthering social reform. By 1945, the coalition's ideological divisions had reasserted themselves, and it proved impossible to extend the life of the government much beyond the defeat of Germany. In the election of July 1945, Labour, catching the electorate's mood, won a landslide victory. Attlee brushed off Herbert Morrison's attempt to insist that the Parliamentary Labour Party approve his acceptance of office (a veiled leadership challenge) and appointed a cabinet full of experienced wartime ministers.

Labour was pledged to a programme of nationalisation and social reform: the Bank of England, the coal and steel industries, civil aviation, electricity and gas supply, the railways, were all taken into state ownership; the main conclusions of Beveridge's famous 1942 report were enacted in the 1946 National Insurance and National Health Service Acts. Confounding the expectations of some of its opponents that Labour's foreign policy would be leftist and overly pro-Soviet, Attlee and his Foreign Secretary, Ernest Bevin, were in fact suspicious of the Soviet Union and keen to cement an alliance between Western Europe and the United States with the creation of the North Atlantic Treaty Organisation in 1949, and through the American's programme of Marshall Aid. To some extent, the search for collective security was designed to replace an empire which was no longer affordable. Attlee hastened British withdrawal from India and Pakistan, and left Burma, Ceylon and Palestine.

After the half-way point the government began to lose steam, battered by crises. Britain's post-war poverty began to bite hard, and the country's trade slid inexorably into deficit. In 1947 the removal of exchange controls (demanded as a condition of an American loan) caused a run on sterling; within a few weeks, they had to be restored. The atmosphere of austerity intensified with the severe winter of 1947-8; a further sterling crisis in 1949 resulted in the devaluation of the pound.

At the General Election of 1950, Labour's majority was cut to five. Britain's commitment to the Korean war added to the difficulties of national finance and helped to irritate a deepening conflict between the right and left wings of the party, represented respectively by Hugh Gaitskell (from October Chancellor of the Exchequer) and Bevan (Minister of Health). The conflict came to a head with Gaitskell's attempt in the run-up to the 1951 budget to impose charges for a number of services which had previously been provided free within the National Health Service; Bevan resigned. Attlee obtained a dissolution of Parliament and brought to an end the painful process of governing with so thin a majority. Although in the General Election Labour polled its highest vote (and a higher percentage than the Conservatives), the Conservative party gained a seventeen-seat victory.

Attlee remained leader of the Labour party for another four years, while the divisions between Bevan and the left on the one hand, and the leadership on the other, became plainer. Attlee tried hard to hold the party together as it argued about German rearmament and further nationalisation. Six months after a second Conservative victory in the General Election of 1955, Attlee retired, aged seventy-two, taking an earldom. Attlee was the least charismatic of men: inscrutable, even gnomic, he sidestepped the great controversies of his party, veiling his own views, and preferred to balance the party factions, rather than stamp his own personality and policy on the party. He died in 1967.

Sir Anthony Eden
1897 – 1977

Anthony Eden was born in 1897, the son of Sir William Eden. His education at Eton was interrupted by the First World War, in which he fought in the King's Royal Rifle Corps, and was awarded the Military Cross. After the war he read Persian and Arabic at Oxford. At Oxford he had been more of an aesthete than a politician; his decision to seek election to Parliament, as a Conservative, came as a surprise to his friends and relatives. He was returned for Warwick and Leamington in 1923. In the same year he married Beatrice Beckett, the daughter of the chairman of the *Yorkshire Post*.

In Ramsay MacDonald's national government of 1931 Eden took his first ministerial post, as Parliamentary Under-Secretary at the Foreign Office under the Liberal, Rufus Isaacs, Marquess of Reading. In 1933 he became Lord Privy Seal, though still attached to the Foreign Office, charged with the British contribution to the Geneva Disarmament Conference. In the summer of 1935, after Baldwin had replaced MacDonald, he brought Eden into the cabinet as Minister for League of Nations affairs. It was an awkward position, designed to signal the government's commitment to the League, but which seemed to set him up as a rival to the incumbent Foreign Secretary, Sir Samuel Hoare. Eden only reluctantly accepted. Hoare in fact destroyed his ministerial career with the Hoare-Laval pact, his attempt to compromise with Mussolini over the invasion of Abyssinia, and after his resignation in December 1935, Eden replaced him, at thirty-eight the youngest to hold the post since Lord Granville.

He took up the office at a moment fraught with tension: in March 1936 Hitler occupied the demilitarised Rhineland; in May Mussolini annexed Abyssinia; in July civil war broke out in Spain; and Germany made formal alliances with both Japan and Italy. Eden was not a determined opponent of appeasement, or an advocate of collective security as Churchill was. Yet after Baldwin's replacement as Prime Minister by Chamberlain he found himself increasingly at odds, not just with Chamberlain's meddlesomeness in foreign affairs, but also with his eagerness to come to terms with the European dictators. In February 1936 he resigned, although even afterwards he and his sympathisers maintained a certain distance from Churchill's attacks on appeasement. Eden accepted Chamberlain's offer to return to the government on the outbreak of the war – albeit in the backwater of the Dominions Office. On Churchill's accession to power, he was moved to be Secretary of State for War, but a few months later, in December 1940, he was restored to the Foreign Secretaryship, and took a place in the war cabinet.

Eden became one of Churchill's closest wartime allies and confidants. The Prime Minister appointed him Leader of the House of Commons in 1942, and as early as 1940 told him that he would be his successor. The relationship was not always an easy one. Churchill and he had disagreements, particularly over Eden's pressing of the case for a greater effort to assist the Soviet Union. Nevertheless, at the 1945 tripartite conference at Yalta (to which he accompanied Churchill, as he did to all the great conferences of the war) he deeply regretted the decision to abandon Poland to Soviet domination.

Eden emerged from the war overworked, tired and ill. His illness coincided with a moment of disillusion about party politics in the face of the enormous sacrifices which had been made. He himself had lost his eldest son, killed in Burma right at the end of the war. In opposition after the Labour victory of 1945, he found little he could disagree on with his successor at the Foreign Office, Ernest Bevin. But after the 1950 election he appeared to recover his stride, and on the Conservatives' return to power in 1951, he went back, once more, to the Foreign Office. These were Eden's best years, on a personal as well as a professional level. His divorce in 1950 was followed by marriage in 1952 to Clarissa Churchill, the Prime Minister's niece. While resisting American pressure for armed intervention in the Far East following the French defeat in Indo-China, Eden helped to avert an American-Chinese confrontation; in the Middle East, though, he succumbed to United States' demands for British decolonisation, withdrawing British forces from Suez in 1954, to the fury of a group of Conservative back benchers and of the Prime Minister himself. Most notably, he rescued NATO from crisis after the French National Assembly's rejection of the European Defence Community, by establishing the more limited European defence cooperation through the Western European Union.

Churchill clung onto office until April 1955 despite a stroke in 1953 and the obvious decline of his powers. Eden himself had again been struck by illness in 1953, but on Churchill's retirement smoothly entered into his long-awaited inheritance of the premiership. With the economy buoyant, Eden fought a General Election within two months, and widened the Conservative lead to sixty, aided by his promise of a 'property-owning democracy', and a tax-cutting budget. Within months, however, the economic boom of the early 1950s had started to go sour. A rise in inflation and a deterioration in the balance of payments forced a deflationary budget and suggested a cabinet reshuffle. R.A. Butler was removed from the Chancellorship and replaced by Harold Macmillan. As Labour experienced something of a renaissance under its new leader, Hugh Gaitskell, the Conservative press mounted a campaign against Eden.

It was an international crisis, however, which dominated Eden's brief premiership. Colonel Nasser had taken over the government of Egypt in a

military coup in 1952; his pan-Arabist rhetoric and courtship of the Soviet bloc
seemed likely to undermine British power in the Middle East. The confrontation
between Nasser and the West came to a head with Nasser's nationalisation of the
Suez canal in July 1956, shortly after the final departure of British troops. With
France, Britain prepared military action to restore the canal to its previous status,
barely hiding their hope that Nasser might suffer as a consequence. But the
United States government regarded military intervention as an overreaction, and
suspected Britain and France of neo-colonial meddling. Its pressure deflected
Eden for the moment from military courses; but when a draft resolution on the
issue was vetoed by the Soviet Union in the United Nations Security Council,
Britain and France returned to considering force. Under the guise of an
intervention against an Israeli attack on the Egyptian frontier they would regain
the canal. Israel's invasion of Egypt took place on 29 October; British and French
troops landed on 5 November. The unfolding of the action produced an
enormous political and diplomatic row. Eden appears to have been taken aback
by the severity of the reaction from Washington, which provoked a run on
sterling, and the operation was stopped a day after it began. President Eisenhower
furiously insisted on complete withdrawal; many Conservative backbenchers
were furious at the retreat. Eden was already ill, and never fully recovered from
the ignominy of the Suez affair. In late November he flew to Jamaica to
recuperate; a few weeks after his return, on 9 January 1957, he resigned.

In 1961 he was created Earl of Avon. The disastrous ending of his
premiership was the culmination of years of successful – at times brilliant –
diplomacy. It was ironic that he was destroyed by actions in the sphere he knew
most about. Eden died in 1977.

Harold Macmillan
1894 – 1986

Harold Macmillan was born in London in 1894, the son of Maurice Macmillan and the grandson of Daniel Macmillan, the founder of the publishing house. His mother, a lively and determined American, dominated his early life. Macmillan was educated at Eton and at Balliol College, Oxford, although his career at the first was truncated by illness and at the second by war. In 1915, a captain in the Grenadier Guards, he received a slight wound at the Battle of Loos; in 1916, at the Somme, he suffered an altogether more serious one which put him out of action for the rest of the war, and from which (had it not been for his mother's determination and influence) he might not have survived. After the war he remained for a time in the army, going to Canada as Aide-De-Camp to the Governor-General, the ninth Duke of Devonshire. Shortly afterwards he married Devonshire's daughter, Lady Dorothy Cavendish.

Macmillan went into the family business; but he was soon aiming for a political career.

In 1924 he won the seat at Stockton-on-Tees, as a rather uncertain Conservative. Part of his political creed had been formed in the trenches, and his paternalistic concern for the working class was confirmed by his experience of representing a north-eastern constituency during the depression: his repudiation of the current Conservative laissez-faire orthodoxy, and, after 1935, his condemnation of appeasement gave him little hope of office under the leadership of either Baldwin or Chamberlain. For a year, in 1936-7, he even resigned his party whip. The war, and Churchill's accession to power brought him in from the cold. He was made Parliamentary Secretary in the Ministry of Supply, and in 1942 moved to the Colonial Office, where he began to think about the position of the British Empire after the war. At the end of the year he gratefully accepted Churchill's offer of the position of Minister Resident at Allied Force Headquarters in North Africa. Macmillan enjoyed the expatriate position immensely, although his task – mediating between the allies in their advance through the Mediterranean and up into Italy, and dealing with the wounded sensibilities of exiled French and Italian politicians – was a complex and even dangerous one. By the end of the war he was Acting President of the Allied Council for Italy, in effect wielding executive power over the whole country, as well as involved in the British attempt to pacify post-war Greece.

Macmillan came down to earth when he returned to Britain. He was appointed Secretary of State for Air in Churchill's pre-election caretaker government, but in the July 1945 Election, a Labour landslide, he lost his Stockton seat. He returned to the Commons at a by-election later the same year. Out of office, Macmillan became one of the spokesmen for a centrist style of Conservatism, an acceptance of Labour's nationalisations and the government's strategic direction of the economy; he also became an enthusiastic advocate of European union. On the Conservatives' resumption of power in 1951, Macmillan accepted the less-than-exciting job of Minister of Housing. Unexpectedly, he found it rather congenial, and made his name with his success in meeting Churchill's pledge of 300,000 new houses a year. There followed grander jobs: Minister for Defence for six months before Churchill's death, and Foreign Secretary for little longer after Eden's arrival as Prime Minister. In December 1955 he became Chancellor of the Exchequer.

Macmillan was among the strongest supporters of Eden's plan to seize the Suez Canal from Nasser, and was closely involved in the planning for the attack; he was also one of the first to recognise that the operation had to be called off when the extent of American fury became clear – allowing Harold Wilson to characterise his position as 'first in, first out'. It did Macmillan no harm, however, for when Eden resigned in January 1957, the cabinet picked him, rather than R.A. Butler (who had had well-publicised doubts about Suez, and who had led the government during Eden's recuperation abroad) as his successor.

Macmillan took office with his party and the country divided over Suez, and with Anglo-American relations at their nadir. The government was not expected to last much more than a few weeks. Yet his renowned 'unflappability' quickly exercised a calming influence over the party, and reduced the febrile atmosphere of the cabinet. Repairing relations with the Americans proved fairly easy for Macmillan, not only half-American himself, but also benefiting from a friendship with President Eisenhower dating from his North African years. The 'special' relationship between the US and the UK became on the one hand a personal relationship between President and Prime Minister (which Macmillan managed to transfer to Eisenhower's successor, John F. Kennedy, in 1961) and on the other a determined pursuit by Britain of nuclear cooperation with America which, Macmillan paradoxically believed, would allow her to retain an independent deterrent and her international status. Macmillan's quest ultimately issued in Kennedy's reluctant agreement to allow Britain to purchase, on generous terms, the new Polaris submarine-launched missile. Macmillan sought to exercise his influence with the Americans to coax them and the Soviet Union into a warmer relationship. He ultimately gained some success with the Nuclear Test Ban Treaty of 1963 which Kennedy attributed to his efforts.

The wooing of America left rather less room for Europe, and Macmillan, like Churchill, had gone cool on the project of European union for which 'the six' had signed up in the Treaty of Rome in 1957, inventing the European Free

Trade Area in 1959 as a rather looser alternative. By the early sixties, however, the European union began – unexpectedly – to seem a workable proposition, and in 1961 Macmillan changed tack and began delicate talks on membership of the European Communities. They were brought abruptly and humiliatingly to an end by the French President de Gaulle's notorious *'non'*, largely because of de Gaulle's suspicions of the closeness of the Anglo-American *entente*. While failing in his attempts to ally with her neighbours, Macmillan set himself to divest Britain of the remnants of its Empire. Macmillan talked of the 'winds of change', and the growth of 'African national consciousness', and indeed, the upswell of nationalism, particularly in the Congo, Rhodesia and Nyasaland required some sort of response; yet the decolonisation of the early 1960s came about largely because of the shrinking of British military spending, and a belief that informal influence could be as effective as possession, and a lot less expensive.

Conservative economic policy had since 1955 been concerned to dampen down growing inflationary pressures; deflationary measures had been extended in 1956 to combat the run on sterling of the Suez crisis. By 1957 they had produced stagnation. The Chancellor, Peter Thorneycroft, was still convinced of the dangers of over-heating, and wanted to continue and extend them: Macmillan disagreed, and phlegmatically accepted the astonishing resignation of the entire Treasury team in January 1958. Thorneycroft's departure paved the way for his successor's dramatic cut in income tax in the 1959 budget, and Macmillan's increased majority in the General Election of October 1959 – although shortly afterwards a sudden economic boom ended in a balance of payments crisis and the brakes were applied in the budgets of 1960 and 1961. The efforts of the new Chancellor, Selwyn Lloyd, to halt wage rises led to confrontations with the public sector unions and contributed to a rapid decline in the government's popularity. After the particularly disastrous by-election at Leicester in the summer of 1962 Macmillan sought to improve the image of his government by sacking and replacing a third of the government, including the Chancellor and the Ministers of Defence, Housing and Education. The 'Night of the Long Knives' failed in its intention. The new Chancellor, Reginald Maudling, reversed the deflationary strategy, attempting a non-inflationary expansion in 1962-3, but the government's by-election performances were no better, and the Profumo affair of 1963 made the government look seedy (although it was vindicated by the inquiry of Lord Denning). Macmillan was already seventy: yet the setbacks did not prevent him from being determined to continue leading the party into the imminent election. Illness, however, did. Taken into hospital for an urgent operation on the eve of the Conservative party conference in October 1963, he was forced to resign.

Macmillan did make a full recovery. Witty and bookish, his languid Edwardian style was widely admired; yet it covered a reserve and shyness, and an enormous capacity for hard work. Macmillan had for many years declined a peerage, and it was not until 1984 that he accepted elevation to the House of Lords as Earl of Stockton. He died in 1986.

1721-42	Sir Robert Walpole (Whig)	1859-65	Viscount Palmerston (Lib)
1742-43	Spencer Compton (Whig)	1865-66	Earl Russell (Lib)
1743-54	Henry Pelham (Whig)	1866-68	Earl of Derby (Con)
1754-56	Duke of Newcastle (Whig)	1868	Benjamin Disraeli (Con)
1756-57	Duke of Devonshire (Whig)	1868-74	William Gladstone (Lib)
1757-62	Duke of Newcastle (Whig)	1874-80	Benjamin Disraeli (Con)
1762-63	Earl of Bute (Tory)	1880-85	William Gladstone (Lib)
1763-65	George Grenville (Whig)	1885-86	Marquess of Salisbury (Con)
1765-66	Marquess of Rockingham (Whig)	1886	William Gladstone (Lib)
1766-67	William Pitt (the Elder) (Whig)	1886-92	Marquess of Salisbury (Con)
1767-70	Duke of Grafton (Whig)	1892-94	William Gladstone (Lib)
1770-82	Lord North (Tory)	1894-95	Earl of Rosebery (Lib)
1782	Marquess of Rockingham (Whig)	1895-1902	Marquess of Salisbury (Con)
1782-83	Earl of Shelburne (Whig)	1902-05	Arthur Balfour (Con)
1783	Duke of Portland (Coalition)	1905-08	Sir Henry Campbell-Bannerman (Lib)
1783-1801	William Pitt (the Younger) (Tory)	1908-16	Herbert Asquith (Lib)
1801-04	Henry Addington (Tory)	1916-22	David Lloyd George (Coalition)
1804-06	William Pitt (the Younger) (Tory)	1922-23	Andrew Bonar Law (Con)
1806-07	Lord Grenville (Whig)	1923-24	Stanley Baldwin (Con)
1807-09	Duke of Portland (Tory)	1924	Ramsay MacDonald (Lab)
1809-12	Spencer Perceval (Tory)	1924-29	Stanley Baldwin (Con)
1812-27	Earl of Liverpool (Tory)	1929-35	Ramsay MacDonald (Lab)
1827	George Canning (Tory)	1935-37	Stanley Baldwin (Nat. Govt)
1827-28	Viscount Goderich (Tory)	1937-40	Neville Chamberlain (Nat Govt)
1828-30	Duke of Wellington (Tory)	1940-45	Winston Churchill (Coalition)
1830-34	Earl Grey (Whig)	1945-51	Clement Attlee (Lab)
1834	Viscount Melbourne (Whig)	1951-55	Winston Churchill (Con)
1834-35	Sir Robert Peel (Tory)	1955-57	Sir Anthony Eden (Con)
1835-41	Viscount Melbourne (Whig)	1957-63	Harold Macmillan (Con)
1841-46	Sir Robert Peel (Tory)	1963-64	Sir Alec Douglas Home (Con)
1846-52	Lord John Russell (Whig)	1964-70	Harold Wilson(Lab)
1852	Earl of Derby (Con)	1970-74	Edward Heath (Con)
1852-55	Earl of Aberdeen (Coalition)	1974-76	Harold Wilson (Lab)
1855-58	Viscount Palmerston (Lib)	1976-79	James Callaghan (Lab)
1858-59	Earl of Derby (Con)	1979-90	Margaret Thatcher (Con)
		1990-	John Major (Con)